PRAISE FOR *ECHOES OF THE EARTH* AND AUTHOR GIL NICHOLS

"*Echoes of the Earth* is a beautifully written book that offers an undeniable connection between centuries-long Indigenous values, and those of Montessori education. Nichols describes the validity of native culture in the context of modern life, particularly through themes of human purpose, value, and individuality within the context of community—all parallel to the values of Montessori education both a century ago, and today. A must-read for Montessorians and all educators."
—Michele Shane, head of school, The Children's House Montessori, Traverse City, Michigan; former president of Montessori Administrators Association; director on the board of AMI/USA

"I met Gil Nichols fifteen years ago when he was on the board of the National Center for Indigenous American Cultures, an organization that served to honor, preserve, and protect the Native heritage of the region and its Native culture and traditions. We have since shared ties to a consortium of urban organizations and participated together in Lakota Sundances, Inipi ceremonies, and other rites. I know Gil to be a very compassionate person and a thoughtful educator who has spent a lifetime seeking to understand Native culture through experience and relationships with Native people and leaders such as Rosebud spiritual leader, Leonard Crow Dog. Gil understands the variety of ways people learn, which equips him to share his expertise and knowledge with others. He is a longtime supporter of the Cheyenne River and Rosebud Reservations, always willing to learn more and 'be a good relative,' (a traditional Indigenous worldview)."
—Gaylene Crouser, Standing Rock Sioux Tribe, executive director, Kansas City Indian Center

"Nowa - My name is Ramona New Rider of the Pawnee Nation. My clan is Skidi. I have had the honor of knowing Gil Nichols for many years. He is indeed a man of character and honor. Our paths came together at CrowDog's Sundance on the Rosebud Indian Reservation, home to the Sicangu Lakota (Burnt Thigh Nation). Our lives flow and

connect through history and ceremonies. Over the years, Gil has supported and embraced Native culture and spirituality. His son Justin was a faithful supporter and head firekeeper for many summers at CrowDog's Paradise and is now a Sundancer on Cheyenne River Reservation. I continue to honor our ceremonial paths together."
—Ramona New Rider, Pawnee Nation, Skidi clan

"I thoroughly enjoyed reading *Echoes of the Earth.* This text was well developed, well documented, and engages the reader in thoughtful contemplation. In full disclosure, Gilbert (Gil) Nichols's path and mine crossed many years ago, well before he wrote this book. I was an impressionable youngster of fifteen when I sat in Mr. Nichols's world history class at Park Hill High School, Kansas City, Missouri. I recognized at the time his penchant for Native American cultures but did not understand the depth of that interest, fascination, and respect. I can reflect on my memories of his class and recall inquiry methods and hypothesis building with clarity. As I read the section, 'Restructuring American Education' I reflected with a grin, this is how Mr. Nichols taught fifty years ago.

"*Echoes of the Earth* provides an engaging and unique view into the lives and traditions of Native Americans. As Nichols provides deep insights into Native American cultures and then draws a parallel look into the current majority culture, he provides the perfect conditions for reflection and deep thought. The author's upbringing, both culturally and geographically, was not particularly different than my own and yet his path took him to extensive study of Native American culture and, after a time, to become a member of the Dakota band through *Hunkakaga*, an adoption ceremony, as he joined the Dion Family on the Dakota Reservation. Whether the topic is governance, agriculture, family structures, or spirituality, an examination of Native American culture provides another perspective worthy of consideration.

"The author shares his vast understanding and deep appreciation of Native American culture with the reader. In a time when governance in our nation is the outcome of a "winner take all" mindset, the Native American tradition of open communication described in the text builds a convincing case for rethinking the way we treat one another in our governance structure. Nichols describes the traditional Native American forum for discussion and consensus building. Discourse, which provides for each individual to speak his or her mind, uninterrupted, until everyone is heard, is so foreign to our bent to speak over one another, I find the concept refreshing. While our majority culture leaders' engagement seems to be to win the issue, the Native Americans' engagement seems to be to win the community. The reality that this sort of commitment to hearing all perspectives may take more time is not a deterrent from being certain all voices are heard.

"Chapter after chapter, example after example, Nichols's words ring true; "As we seek answers to today's problems, I propose that Native America offers a model that may provide solutions to our current challenges." Included in the section "Native American Contributions" is an impressive list and description of agricultural items and techniques. Included in the section "Finding New Solutions," Native cultures suggest a child who is nurtured from the inside out, rather than the outside in, (being told what to do) can grow into being the person she/he is meant to become.

"The importance of family structure is pervasive throughout the culture and thus the implications of that importance are manifested throughout the text. Fascinating and important tenets, fundamental to Native America, unfold in the section "Native Spirituality." For instance, the notion of power as it relates to how much one can give rather than how much one can collect is integral to the belief that there is no connection between true power and materialism.

Each page is filled with insights and thought-provoking metaphors. As one turns to the next page, they are greeted with yet another enlightening insight. I recommend this text to those with an open mind and a curiosity about Native American cultures. I am eager to see the final release of *Echoes of the Earth* and will be certain to secure this work for our school library, the school in which I am currently the principal; the school in which I first had the opportunity to learn about Native culture from Gil Nichols."

—Brad Kincheloe, PhD, principal, Park Hill High School, Kansas City, Missouri

Echoes of the Earth

Indigenous Wisdom for Modern Challenges

GILBERT G. NICHOLS

MISSION POINT PRESS

Readers are encouraged to go to www.MissionPointPress.com to contact the author, or to contact the publisher about how to buy this book in bulk at a discounted rate.

Mission Point Press

Published by Mission Point Press
2554 Chandler Rd.
Traverse City, MI 49696
(231) 421-9513
www.MissionPointPress.com

Design by Sarah Meiers

Softcover ISBN: 978-1-965278-32-1
Hardcover ISBN: 978-1-965278-33-8

Library of Congress Control Number: 2024925875

Printed in the United States of America

Dedicated to:

My sons, Anthony Craig Nichols and Justin Lloyd Nichols.

And to the Native Community who accepted me and took me beyond the written word.

Diane and Nuelin Dion (Ihaŋktoŋwaŋ Dakota)

Leonard Crowdog (Sicangu Oyate Lakota)

Archie Fire Lame Deer (Miniconjou/Sicangu Lakota)

Unci (Grandma) Chipps (Sicangu Oglala Lakota)
and her son Godfrey Chipps (Oglala Lakota)

Grandpa Fools Crow (Oglala Lakota)

I could never reach their depth, but I am so grateful they led me on a ZUYA (lifelong journey) I'm still traveling and learning.

TABLE OF CONTENTS

Upon suffering beyond suffering, the Red Nation shall rise again, and it shall be a blessing in a sick world. A world filled with broken promises, selfishness and separations. A world longing for the light again.

Tȟašúŋke Witkó (Crazy Horse)

PREFACE

If you want the present to be different from the past, study the past.

—Baruch Spinoza

When I was six years old, my family moved into a ten-story apartment building in Midtown Kansas City, Missouri, at the intersection where 35th Street (Amour Boulevard) Ts with Broadway. I considered that building my home until I left for college. About three hundred people lived there. It covered a fifth of a city block, including a small parking lot for only about eight cars, since most residents used public transportation. There were brownstones in the neighborhood as well as taller residential buildings.

I remember one day, sitting on a retaining wall at the side of the building, wondering why we were living in a place so full of noise and confusion. There was constant, never-ending traffic, with cars seemingly going nowhere. I thought, *What are all these people doing here? If I had a car, I would not be here.*

When I was a freshman in college, that question "Why are we here?" remained, though in a broader sense. I have been seeking answers ever since.

Paradoxically, it was out of that urban environment in early childhood that I became fascinated by Native America, much to the growing chagrin of the adults in my life. I have experienced resistance to my interest in Native America all my life. But Native America has become a part of me.

Some 40 years ago, I was adopted into a family from the Ihanktonwan Dakota reservation in Lake Andes, South Dakota. During the adoption process, I was honored with a name originating from that Native family's ancestor. Years later, during a ceremony, a medicine person received spiritual instruction to give me an additional name expressed in Lakota. Indigenous names are not merely pronouns; they possess metaphorical depth, reflecting one's relationship to spiritual forces and "the big picture." Their meaning deepens with experience and age, and they are only used in a spiritual context, which is why I don't share them here.

My adoption permanently altered the course of my life journey. This book reflects not only my personal history with Native America but also my academic background.

As a college student, I was most drawn to the social sciences. Historiography sparked my interest in critical approaches to research, and Advanced Cultural Anthropology broadened my horizons even further, proving to be one of the most thought-provoking and challenging classes of my education.

As I gained more tools with which to view the world, a problem became increasingly present in my mind. When I examined the relationship between Euro-Americans and Native America from an academic perspective, I realized that the staggering violence and othering Native Americans suffered at the hands of the colonizers continued long after we are taught it had ended. Only now, the injustice was perpetrated in history books instead of with muskets.

Agnotology, the study of deliberate, culturally induced

distortions and half-truths, is a critical concept in the social sciences. Written and taught history is often distorted based on one's biases, background, and motivations. And it is difficult to overstate the level of historical distortion inflicted on Native American peoples by Euro-American bias.

That begs the question: What were the Indigenous cultures really like in 1492?

Most of our sources of information come from European accounts. For example, when I read European accounts of the Aztecs, or Mexica (pronounced *Mashica*), human sacrifice is almost always highlighted.

This is an example of historical bias that has been passed down through generations. It exposes an "us and them" attitude that highlighted human sacrifice in other cultures but ignored similar behavior among their own people. Research has exposed the massive numbers of human sacrifice that took place in Europe during the Reformation. For example, when I visited an Italian town near the Swiss border, I discovered information about the women who had been burned at the stake there. There were numbers and dates listed of their execution, but their names were omitted. Some 40,000 women were burned at the stake for witchcraft over about 80 years during the last half of the 16th and first half of the 17th centuries. Interestingly, only 10,000 men met the agony of the fire. In Spain, the number of executions was so large they used platforms instead of single-stake execution. Critical thinking reveals that the Spanish obsession with Indigenous sacrifice, while turning a blind eye to their own atrocities, was and is nothing short of xenophobic hypocrisy.

While correcting the blind spots of history is important, its significance extends beyond matters of justice for the centuries of lies and misperceptions inflicted on Native Americans.

It is a matter of survival.

A lifelong study of European history reveals patterns of conflict—horrific wars, domination, environmental destruction, corruption, and greed. These patterns trace all the way back to the earliest formation of nation-state socio-political systems, and they continue, unerringly, to the present day.

These patterns of destruction have been so prevalent that it would be easy to assume they are simply a part of human nature. But are they? Or could the self-destructive spiral we find ourselves in be a consequence of misdirected human socio-political constructs?

In my studies, I have found key elements seriously lacking in our discourse of history. One glaring omission is the destruction caused by masculine domination and the absence of proper restraint from the feminine aspect of our nature.

In contrast, the North American Indigenous cultures that encountered the colonists were societies without class distinctions. They operated with a balance of feminine and masculine principles in their socio-political systems, making them more inclusive in their attitudes and behaviors compared to the more exclusive thought processes of the Euro-Americans.

In terms of armed conflict, the difference between cultures is equally stark. Before Europeans arrived in North America, no Native culture had a standing army, police force, jails, or prisons. Their conception of warfare generally involved raiding another peoples, not clashes between huge armies, as was the case in Europe. And the difference isn't due to differences in population sizes; demographers today estimate pre-Columbian populations north of the Rio Grande River numbered around 20 million.

The Native American peoples discussed in Euro-American history books had already been decimated by disease. Demographers estimate that as many as 90% of Native peoples died from diseases introduced by Euro-Americans. The highest death rates occurred among the healthiest individuals, as their antibodies overreacted to the diseases, leaving the elderly helpless and dying of starvation. It was disaster for Indigenous communities.

European disease brought devastation, and Euro-American military forces and militias did the rest. By 1900, U.S. population statistics reveal that of the once 20 million Native Americans, only 250,000 were left in the U.S. as a result of the Euro-American invasion.

Yet it was the Euro-Americans who considered themselves the "civilized" peoples.

As Walter Benjamin, German Jewish philosopher, cultural critic, and essayist wrote, "There is no document of civilization which is not at the same time a document of barbarism." Given all the wars brought on by the rise and fall of civilizations, and the brutality colonists have inflicted on the colonized, Walter Benjamin's quote raises some interesting questions about the true nature of what we call "civilized."

And now more than ever, our civilization is revealing its true nature, and it is self-destructive. On Wednesday, January 6, 2021, President Donald J. Trump held a rally about a mile from the U.S. Capitol building, claiming the election had been stolen from him and inciting thousands of rioters, who then marched on the Capitol. A shocked nation watched the ensuing desecration. The mob left millions of dollars in destruction, five people dead (two women and three men, one a capitol police officer) and many more injured. Two more capitol police officers later committed suicide.

This destabilization is only the beginning. If we stay the course, if we fail to learn alternative methods of politics, value systems, education, and ways to cultivate a sustainable relationship with the environment, how can we hope to survive?

Interestingly, from ancient times to Putin's invasion of Ukraine, we can see in *Macbeth* Shakespeare's metaphorical reflections on the arc of nation-state history.

After living a life corrupted by ambition, Macbeth's wife's death led him to question the meaning of life, comparing it to a fleeting shadow moving through time and space before vanishing, to be "heard no more." And if life is meaningless, then his obsessive pursuit of power appears all the more depraved. Life becomes an unfulfilled trap for those consumed by the illusion of power.

This book explores the tension between blind ambition and objectification, as seen in *Macbeth,* and the importance of relationship, which reflects the Native American way of viewing existence. Macbeth's behavior represents the negative potential of nation-state patterns. Macbeth says of life:

> *Life is but a walking Shadow,*
> *A poor player that struts and*
> *Frets his hour upon the stage and*
> *Then is heard no more. It is a tale told*
> *By an idiot, full of sound and fury*
> *Signifying nothing.*

In contrast to the self-destructive, pointless fury represented by the nation-state paradigm, I am reminded of a Native American Blackfoot death song:

> *What is life? It is the flash of the firefly at night. It is the breath of a buffalo in the wintertime. It is the little shadow that runs across the prairie and loses itself in the sunset.*

These words accept nature as it is rather than trying to manipulate it. It puts human life in perspective, within a network of relationships, rather than the ego-driven paradigm of "man above." It reflects a value system based on connection instead of separation and greed.

As we seek answers to today's problems, I propose that Native America offers a model that may provide solutions to our current challenges. By studying both Western and Indigenous cultures, we can weave the best qualities of each into a sustainable paradigm and pathway for the future.

To make that case, I will first introduce the Axial Age patterns and paradigms to explain how the world arrived at its current state. Then, I will closely examine traditional Native North American cultures and the solutions they might offer. The purpose of this book is not to establish absolutes, but to open the door to further contemplation.

Until we confront our history and seriously examine Native cultures, we may struggle to resolve the issues we face today. A new pathway brings uncertainty and fear, but along this journey through life, we grow and expand. By merging the distinct cultural constructs of Indigenous peoples in this hemisphere with the current nation-state paradigm, we can discover potential solutions to our current challenges.

It is time to embrace our full humanity, moving beyond a purely technological view of progress. To achieve this, we must first examine the patterns underlying our history.

CHAPTER 1

THE AXIAL PATTERNS THAT FOSTER EXTERNAL DESTRUCTION AND IMPLOSION

We do not yet know whether the attack on the Capitol will be replicated or become part of a pattern.

Barbara F. Walter, *How Civil Wars Start: And How to Stop Them*

Today, America is at a crossroads. To look forward for solutions, we must first look back to identify the core issues and patterns that brought us to this point. As I watch the daily newscasts and talk to friends and neighbors, one thing is clear: America has a blind spot when it comes to understanding the deeper meanings reflected in history. Only if this blind spot is corrected can we begin to explore solutions to today's dangerous socio-political problems.

Axial Age Nation-state Patterns

It's easy to look at historic events as isolated snapshots, disconnected by moments in time. But if we take a longer view, patterns emerge.

The German philosopher/historian Karl Jaspers and others defined the period of 2800 to 2200 BP (Before Present) as the Axial Age. During this period, Greece, India, Iran, the Levant (the region now consisting of Syria, Lebanon, Israel, Jordan, and Palestine), and China emerged as distinct nations with defined borders and national identities.

Nation-state socio-political systems had developed previously, but what is significant about this period is that it can be seen as the headwaters of a metaphorical river where earlier empires, like Babylon and Egypt, would join as tributaries flowing into the 21st century.

The Axial Age marks a watershed moment in the rising world dominance of nation-state socio-political systems and patterns. It gives us a paradigm through which to understand that the current world is a human construct—not human nature. The flow from past to present is steady and consistent, and it inevitably ends in the decline of the nation-state.

Axial Anchor Points

What touched the shores of this hemisphere when Columbus arrived in 1492 was 4,000 years of nation-state evolutionary development. Mesopotamia had seen the emergence of Eridu, Uruk, and Ur, eventually melding into Babylonia, with the first laws in human history appearing under the reign of the Babylonian King Hammurabi. Thus began the Axial patterns we are faced with today. They have repeated again and again since 2800–2200 BC. And each time, from the decline and fall of the Greek Macedonian, Roman, and the Mongolian empires to the decline and end of the British Empire after World War II, they have ended in collapse.

To secure America's future, these are the patterns we must address if we are to stop the inevitable outcome that history has demonstrated repeatedly. What are the patterns?

1. **Formation of borders that intensify the binary distinction of "them and us"**

   Babylonia

   "Civilization" begins with the rise of city-states such as Sumer c. 5000–3300 BP. Eventually, the Sumerian city-states began to merge with the Akkadians, forming the world's first empire in that region. The seeds for the first nation-state identity, Babylonia, were planted. Under the rule of Hammurabi (1792–1750 BC), and through military force, Babylonia expanded to control all of Mesopotamia. That expansion intensified a sense of nation-state identity, fostering a consciousness of "them and us."

   Egypt

   The 18th dynasty of ancient Egypt (1550–1292 BC) exemplifies a "them and us" mentality both internally and externally. Under Pharaoh Amenhotep III, Egypt reached its furthest expansion, stretching from Sudan to Syria through the military conquest of "them," and strengthening its national identity—"us." Later, Amenhotep's son Pharaoh Amenhotep IV changed his prenomen (Egyptian throne name) to Akhenaten and moved the capital of Egypt from Thebes to Armana. In doing so, he shifted the religious center away from Amun Ra to a new religion centered on the god Aten, associated with his new name, Akhenaten. This distanced him from the powerful priest of Amun Ra and his supporters. But the end result was a division between followers of the new and old religions. When Akhenaten's son Tutankhaten became Pharaoh, he moved the capital back to Thebes and changed his prenomen to Tutankhamun, restoring the godhead Amun Ra. The internal "them and us" of Akhenaten's new religion thus failed, stabilizing Egypt.

Rome

The rise of the Roman Empire provides another example. The empire's expansion cost the lives of 100 million people and enslaved another 20 million to sustain its economy. Its legions spread the empire around the Mediterranean, up through Gaul, and into the British Isles. It attempted several times over 28 years to cross the Rhine River and conquer Germania but was largely unsuccessful, never establishing long-term control over the Germanic tribes. The Germanic "them" defeated the legions of both Emperor Augustus and Emperor Tiberius, driving Augustus into deep depression. In 410, the Visigoths sacked the city of Rome, and the Western Roman Empire collapsed in 476. The eastern half of the empire, Byzantine, struggled on, but was invaded by "them"—the Turkish Ottoman Empire—who conquered it in 1453. It provided yet another example of how the paradigm of the nation-state cannot be sustained.

Present Day

The same "us and them" pattern continues in the U.S. today. Examples include the issues at our southern border and in the nation's political parties. This is why it's so important to recognize and address the pattern rather than focusing on specific incidents or people.

2. **Objectification of "the other"**

The second pattern inherent to nation-states that leads to eventual destruction is the dehumanization of the "other." Belief systems emerge to justify and intensify discrimination, sexism, and tyranny within nation-states. These systems foster strong ego-driven personalities that evolve from leadership to authoritarianism. Examples include:

Enslavement

The Euro-American enslavement of Africans who were sold for profit is a horrific example of the objectification of others. Native Americans were also sold into slavery.

Caste system of India

For centuries, Untouchables have lived substandard lives in which they served other castes. This system continues today.

Missing and murdered Indigenous women

Today, well over 5,000 Native American women disappear or are murdered each year. One reason behind this is the objectification of Indians who were placed on reservations as settlers took their land without compensating them. Native

American Indigenous people became "the other"—lesser Americans.

Putin's Nazi-Jews claim as justification for invading Ukraine

Russia has captured the Donbas, the region of eastern Ukraine with the greatest economic value. Putin justified this by saying he was saving the inhabitants, whom he claimed considered themselves Russian and were under attack from an invasion of "Nazi-Jews," a contradictory stereotype.

Wars

Once borders form, the next step is to defend and expand them. Wars follow this trend. From Hammurabi to Alexander the Great to World Wars I and II to the current war in Ukraine, war is an Axial pattern.

3. **The redefinition of power from the spiritual to the physical and the shift to pyramidal governing structure**

Historian Richard Tarnas defines spirituality as "undifferentiated participatory," a direct spiritual connection with no intermediary like the church. As nation-states emerge, authority shifts from egalitarian clans (extended families) with advisory chiefdoms, to a head of state. To sustain authority, a leader becomes associated with the God complex, either as a half-god, as in ancient Egypt, or as one chosen by a god, such as the long-ruling Capetian dynasty of France. Eventually, leadership evolves from having an association with a godhead to a secular leader, beginning in Europe with Napoleon Bonaparte. One often hears that the most powerful person in the world is the president of the United States. This is in direct opposition to the spiritual concept of power.

Pyramidal Structure

Once nation-states form borders, organizational patterns become pyramidal, with royalty, a dictator, or a president/prime minister at the top. This pyramidal structure fosters a tendency toward top-down dictatorial forms of governance and flows through a chain of command as the pyramid widens toward the bottom. Any pyramidally organized democracy is vulnerable to the rise of authoritarianism.

4. **Power defined by materialism, leverage, wealth, and expansion**

Once nation-states are formed, the definition of power shifts from spiritual forces to material status and the ability to manipulate through force, leverage, and influence. Examples include:

Genghis Kahn: Kahn conquered the largest land-based empire in the history of the world. His armies overtook China, central Asia, the middle East, Russia, and parts of eastern Europe.

Mercantilism: The English became the most efficient at applying the economic theory that defines power as wealth, measured in gold, silver, or natural resources that could be bought and sold. They developed the first industrial revolution in furniture production by depleting the forests of New England and the East Coast. They established favorable leverage in trade, causing other countries to pay them in gold and silver.

Brazil: The largest rainforest in the world, which produces 20% of the world's oxygen, is being cut down for individual and national profit. Past President Bolsonaro declared that the Amazon belongs to Brazil and claimed he was fulfilling a mission from God to harvest it. He also announced he would open protected Indigenous reserves to mining.

5. **Wealth and property-based class structure**
Historically, those who owned the land ruled the land. During the Industrial Revolution, this shifted to capital acquisition. Examples include:

Athens

Often credited with being the first democracy, that democracy had limitations. The right to vote was restricted to male property owners who could trace their pure Athenian blood back five generations. Those who could not participate included slaves, metics (foreigners living in Athens for business reasons), women, and Athenians who did not own property.

America's Gilded Age

The 19th century elite were industrialists who became known as "robber barons" that built huge fortunes as "captains of industry." These included J.P. Morgan, Henry Ford, and others.

American corporations today

The Supreme Court's ruling in Citizens United gave American corporations the right to freedom of speech under the First Amendment of the Constitution. This paved the way to unlimited political donations and vastly increased their political power. But corporations are not individuals. They are production machines who answer to their leaders and shareholders. And their priority is profit, not democracy.

6. **The rise of institutionalization**

The pattern of nation-state governance tends to serve the wealthy class. Even in a republic like the U.S., the issue of institutionalization remains persistent. Institutions created to serve the people tend to evolve toward serving those in power. This was true of the 17th and 18th century English Parliament in the struggle between the Whigs and the Tories, and it is true of today's American House of Representatives. We see it also in the tendency of democracies to succumb to authoritarianism, as in Adolf Hitler's takeover of the Weimar Republic and Alexander Lukashenko's rule in Belarus.

7. **Masculine domination**

As nation-states evolve, another emerging pattern is masculine dominance. Examples include the evolution of the Cycladic pregnant goddess of the Aegean Sea (3200–1100 BC) into the armor-clad Athena of the Parthenon (447–438

BC). We see it also in the British right of progeniture and the all-male presidents of the United States. Women who achieve positions of power within a nation-state must conform to masculine norms in order to achieve that status. Ambition has become a necessary quality for success, seen positively in men ("he's focused and going somewhere") but considered negative in women ("she's aggressive, harsh").

8. Controlled child-rearing

Once borders were created, children were raised and educated to support the nation-state systems. When the universities of Oxford (ca. 1096) and Cambridge (1209) were established, formal education included religion, philosophy, the arts, and history, and was primarily patronized by the upper class. Industrialization's need for a more educated workforce intensified and broadened curriculums during the Industrial Revolution, as it increasingly focused on preparing students for the industrialized future. Industrialization also imposed a new developmental stage, adolescence, to keep children in school longer to prepare them for the workforce. This fostered a societal and parenting process of outside-in, authoritarian, control-based education. Children who did not fit the mold experienced failure in the United States. The European model directed those students into the trades as they entered adolescence. For the past 50 years, American education has focused increasingly on technology and job skills, frequently at the cost of the arts, social sciences, and the development of critical thinking skills.

9. Abstract ideologies and the growth of illegitimate abstract ideologies

Western culture has been on a path to understand the universe since the Greek philosopher Democritus (460–370 BC) proposed an atomic theory of the universe. Later, Sir Isaac Newton introduced the concept of interval time, shifting the focus to linear progression and establishing science as a distinct discipline from philosophy. Newton's inductive reasoning intellectually separated man from nature, marking a tipping point in the evolution toward a mentality of humans as dominant over nature, a shift that institutionalized religion had already begun by worshiping a deity instead of nature. After Newton, our consciousness shifted toward the abstract, supporting the development of abstract ideologies in human thought. Fragmented linear thought began to dominate our worldview, and the oneness of the universe faded from general human conscience. This, in turn, opened the floodgates to dangerous and abstract ideologies, such as Manifest Destiny, racial stereotyping, and the January 6 attack on the U.S. Capitol.

10. Linear time equals progress

History is generally written as a consecutive series of events in narrative form. This results in a distortion caused by a lack of contextual perspective. Once humanity accepted the idea of measuring time in intervals, change became equated with progress. This narrowed the definition of progress to primarily technological advancements, and led to the misguided concepts of "primitive" and "civilized." European invaders justified foreign conquest with an egotistic attitude of superiority, giving them the right to conquer, colonize, and steal foreign homelands and resources around the world. Human understanding of time became linear, obscuring recognition of a flow that included cyclical patterns.

11. **Acceptability of manipulation for political gain**
    Internal political dissention was present all the way back to ancient Egyptian, Babylonian, and Assyrian civilizations. Once the pyramidal socio-political structure of government developed, political corruption emerged as a repeating pattern based on the increasing primacy of ambition. Over time, this has taken many forms. Examples include the execution of Socrates and Henry VIII's defiant formation of the Anglican church when the Pope refused to grant him an annulment from Catherine of Aragon. We see this today in Xi Jinping's total control of China and Putin's control of Russia.

12. **Justification through superiority**
    Aggressor societies justify their actions. In the case of colonization, the Europeans projected their values and perspectives onto the Indigenous cultures, discounting what they really were at their core. The film industry has also created a romanticized and agnotological distortion that fosters ignorance, bias, and doubt. This has fostered an American mentality of Indigenous inferiority and irrelevance, reinforced by an educational system that rarely highlights the original peoples of this land.

    Nation-state societies claim to be driven by practicality.

> But until we put events in proper context, we cannot justify such claims. We need to view events in a broader, more comprehensive perspective to reveal the larger patterns and long-term outcomes of nation-states. Focusing on current politics or events obscures the patterns they represent and desensitizes us to the human suffering they cause. As history has shown, "us and them" justification eventually turns in on itself, as we see in the growing distrust and animosity between the two political parties in the United States.

Native societies were organized in an entirely different paradigm. In nation-state political systems, "no man is above the law." In traditional Native America, no individual, woman or man is above the law of nature. The next eight chapters describe tribal systems that predated the nation-state patterns listed above.

Those systems held wisdom and solutions that can help us today.

CHAPTER 2

THE INDIGENOUS PARADIGM

The idea of progress has relied ... on the lack of a clear vision of the distant past.... As anthropologists have taken a closer and less anthropocentric look at hunter-gatherers, the evidence has shown that "primitives" ... led a surprisingly humane existence.

—Andrew B. Schmookler, Ph.D.

Most information about the native cultures that Europeans encountered when they first arrived in the Western Hemisphere comes from European accounts. A closer and perhaps broader look at tribal life in North America before the European invasion reveals a different view of the healthy, sophisticated cultures that existed in North America before 1492 and the founding of Jamestown in 1607.

Process Orientation

Native Americans did have goals, but they existed to give

direction; the important part was the process. For example, the annual Lakota Sundance was—and still is—a process in which the dance serves as the path to spiritual connection. A sacrifice is made for the health and well-being of the community, not the dancer; although in the end, because we are all one, the dancer benefits as well. "In Aboriginal philosophy, existence consists of energy," Leroy Little Bear, Blackfoot researcher and professor emeritus at the University of Lethbridge, explains. "All things are animate, imbued with spirit, and in constant motion. In this realm, interrelationships between all entities are of paramount importance, and space is a more important referent than time."

The Sundancer is not there for ego. It is because of the interrelationship mentioned above that the sacrifice is made for community, not self. John Archibald Wheeler, the American theoretical physicist, sees this "interrelationship" as more aligned with reality than the thought processes dominating Western thought. He observed: "Scientists are discovering a truth Indians have known all along, that the world is entire and whole, indivisible. It is not 'out there,' but inseparable from ourselves" (Grinde and Johansen, 2008, 218).

These quotes reveal a major inconsistency in some Euro-American analysis. For example, there are scholars who, in their examination of the Native American mound building cultures, project a Euro-American interpretation into the Indigenous mind. In Europe, to build that type of structure, a pyramidal organization paradigm—a chain-of-command—was used. But Indigenous cultures were not European, and their leadership was not dictatorial. The mounds reflect a flow of energy that represents the powerful sense of community embodied in the Sundance, standing in direct contrast to the Euro-American egoic mindset.

Native cultures embraced equality and spirituality of oneness in all that is. They gave thanks to the trees for the gift of housing and air, and the plants and animals for the gift of sustenance, viewing them as equal partners in the universe. This reveals a sense of homogeneity between all that is, including humanity, which contrasts sharply with the spiritual traditions of the Euro-American invader. Ned Blackhawk, in his book *The Rediscovery of America*, explains Indigenous knowledge this way: "Indigenous knowledge explained the composition of the universe and offered lessons on how to survive within it. This was knowledge that gave meaning to everyday life and linked spiritual and earthly realms in song, kinship and stories" (2023, 118).

Indigenous consciousness did not perceive or respond to a dictatorial chain of command, instead responding to norms and mores. That is why law and police were unnecessary in these tribal communities.

A comparison between Indigenous and European linguistics is revealing. Indigenous languages assume a flow of energy through oneness and relationships, while European languages reflect a more categorical thought process. When examining the Indigenous thought process and its perspective of oneness, is it logical to assume the existence of a hierarchy in Indigenous authority? Or was it more of a cooperative understanding that functioned efficiently in an egalitarian society, where norms and mores created close relationships between people and nature?

Many scholars today posit that, as recently as the last hundred years, the world "has experienced the greatest expansion of freedom and political rights in the history of mankind" (Walter, 2022, 9).

But is this actually the case?

Euro-American historians are biased to focus only on the history of nation-states. But humans existed long before that. Paleoanthropologists now believe that *Homo sapiens sapiens* evolved in northern Africa around 300,000 years ago, earlier than what I learned in school. The Neanderthals went extinct about 40,000 years ago, leaving *Homo sapiens sapiens* as the only two-legged species for thirty-five thousand years before the formation of nation-states. In other words, seven-eighths of our history was lived without competition from other hominins, before the rise of Sumer, Babylonia, Egypt, and Norte Chico of Peru. (Norte Chico, also known as Caral-Supe (ca. 3500–1800 BC), is the oldest known "civilization" in the Americas, containing several cities along the Pacific coast and inland. Extensive research of the area has revealed no weapons of war and no chain of command to date.)

Euro-American historians have a bias toward the past 12.5% of our history, when there was no competition from other hominins. They also tend to overlook tribal histories, many of which were recorded, for example, in petroglyphs and winter counts used by tribal historians of the plains. South of the U.S. border, some peoples—such as the Maya—had libraries full of codices. The Spanish destroyed the majority, deeming them works of the devil. It is time we move past our historical denial and examine other valid human constructs, such as tribalism.

Upon their first arrival in this hemisphere, Europeans found the unfamiliar landscapes, peoples, and cultures to be alien. Be it out of ignorance, projection, or self-interest, they created an image of Indigenous inferiority that has continued into the present.

Those early Europeans examined the Indigenous peoples from a materialistic perspective, remaining blind to the Indigenous development of a pharmacological knowledge far beyond that of any nation-state in the world. They did not see that Native America was made up of consensus-building egalitarian democracies with the world's most extensive agricultural development. These innovative human advancements were invisible to the Europeans who equated advancement with castles, knights in metal breast plates, cathedrals, and gunpowder. The native inhabitants aligned with the earth's natural processes in rhythmic motion, not man above—a perspective unimaginable to the colonizers.

As the new arrivals expanded onto Indigenous lands, many ignored or were unaware of the scholarly writings of individuals such as Roger Williams, Thomas Paine, and Ben Franklin, as well as the European Enlightenment movement, which took a more objective view of Indigenous cultures. The early works of Roger Williams (1603–1683) and debatably even Thomas Paine (1737–1809) in the colonial period were among the first European attempts to see through the Native eye.

In North America, tribal people were governed by lineage-based consensus-building democracies for thousands of years. And the foundational consciousness of those democracies was, as theoretical physicist John Wheeler stated above, a "participatory universe … not 'out there,' but inseparable from ourselves." That explains why in tribal societal systems, norms and mores operated in inclusive unison with the governing principles of the universe, making personal material possession minimal and law enforcement unnecessary. In contrast, nation-states do not operate in that "participatory universe," as illustrated by the intense and numerous international conflicts that have repeated since their formation, as well as environmental destruction resulting in climate change.

I am reminded of the deadly issues involving Hamas and Israel and the resulting, sometimes dangerous demonstrations on U.S. college campuses in response. Law enforcement has attempted to lessen the dangers caused by the demonstrations. This represents an example of the problems involved in that separation from a "participatory universe." The human mind begins a shift from thinking in terms of relativity to a binary framework of either/or, good versus evil.

The Euro-American mentality projected aggression on a people who were far less competitive and far more interactive with their neighbors than the Europeans were, and much of our history reflects that. The linear-binary view could not comprehend that the dominant inter-tribal process was cooperative, not conflict intensive. The cooperative ethos resulted in and fostered highly developed oratory skills among the Indigenous leadership.

Tribal nations were far more likely to negotiate and trade both material items and ideas than to engage in conflict. For example, the agricultural areas of lower New England had strong trading relationships with tribes located in Canada, where growing seasons were much shorter, thus creating a well-rounded diet among the more northern tribes. Relations could also be solidified through inter-tribal marriage.

Confederacies were formed for inter-tribal cooperation, not for defense, as was the case in Europe. Tribal peoples identified with territories but not borders. That was true until, further south, the Tsenacommacah Confederacy and alliances rapidly expanded due to concerns over Spanish aggression.

The foundational principles of tribal ethos were sustainability and relationships. They established guardrails for tribal aggression. Wheeler's quote about a participatory universe goes a long way in explaining why native peoples were less aggressive. Until the chaos brought on by the European invasion, conflicts among native peoples were limited.

Tribal constructs and spirituality mitigated human conflict, a lesson worth examining given the almost constant conflict in today's world, including the crisis in Ukraine and current high urban crime rates. It should not be forgotten, the U.S. pulled out of Afghanistan after 20 years of conflict. Excluding the losses in Iraq over this period, the U.S. lost 2,401 military lives and another 20,752 were wounded in action. Eighteen Central Intelligence Agency operatives also died in Afghanistan. Those who returned home often suffer lifelong physical and psychological disabilities, including loss of limbs and PTSD.

In order to gain desperately needed perspective on today's nation-state dilemmas, we must broaden our view of human potential. The current perspective of some scholars, as mentioned previously, is far too narrow, as is the concept of progress, which focuses only on materialistic improvements rather than on improving our humanity. Ever-increasing mass shootings with rapid-fire weapons leaving innocent victims injured and dead must end. A good starting point is to end the illusion that "time equals progress." The universe does not operate by that concept, as quantum physicists have pointed out.

The purpose of this book is to bring reality back into the discussion about the native peoples of this hemisphere, with emphasis on North America.

Native Egalitarianism

Euro-Americans eliminated the true meaning of native egalitarianism. They also trivialized and demeaned native women with the word "squaw," a distortion of the Algonquin word for a woman's sexuality. That sense of feminine insignificance was a projection of the Euro-American mentality with which American women have enduringly struggled against to obtain equal rights.

The original peoples of this land did not think in those terms. Egalitarianism best describes the presence of equality between the feminine and masculine in North American Indigenous populations. Both matrilineal and patrilineal tribes maintained egalitarian roles.

One example is the patrilineal Anishinaabe societies of the Great Lakes region. The Anishinaabe/Ojibwe word *mindimooyenh* translates to "one who holds things together," which refers to a female Elder. It evokes the autonomy of women in Ojibwe society as healers, clan consensus builders, and managers of *manoomin* (wild rice), an ancient food staple of the Great Lakes tribes.

An excellent source on this subject is Red Lakes Ojibwe author and professor Brenda Child, whose book published in 2010, *Holding Our World Together: Ojibwe Women and the Survival of Community*, takes readers through the historic role and challenges of Ojibwe women. In their language, clans were called *doodem.* Child states, "An Ojibwe writer interprets the term *doodem* to mean *that from which I draw my purpose, meaning and being*" (29). In the *doodems*, women and men were economically and socially equal and "… their clan system was one that encouraged fluidity and the possibility of new partnerships and connections between peoples" (32). She goes on to explain that wives and husbands did not lose their original clan identity, which facilitated more flexibility in relationships. In fact, "Ojibwe men were expected to hunt for their in-laws during the period of amity that is the first year of marriage" (35). This provided a sense of egalitarian balance in the intra-tribal ethos and social network of the Anishinaabe patrilineal system.

Numerous forces contributed to the creation of an illegitimate historical account of the original peoples of this land. Undoubtedly, much of the myth originated during colonial times, either as a complete misunderstanding of vastly different cultures or as a rationalization for colonial aggression and the need for domination.

Even Indigenous children were not spared. To "kill the Indian, save the man," native children were taken from their families and placed in "boarding schools" from 1879 until, in many cases, the 1960s. Some states still ignore the Indian Child Welfare Act of 1978 meant to keep children with their culture by allowing adoption into non-Indigenous families. (Native boarding schools existed as early as colonial times, but more recently, children were forcibly taken from their homes.) These schools, of which there were over four hundred in the U.S., attempted to rob children of their Indigenous heritage. They forbade the speaking of native languages, and those who broke that rule were severely punished. In fact, the schools have graveyards full of children who did not survive their time there. Parents who hid their children were punished by the U.S. government. In 1895, Hopi resistors were even charged with sedition and imprisoned at Alcatraz for a year.

Even today, Native American children still struggle to obtain an accurate view of their ancestral history. The U.S. Department of Education has delegated to the states control of the curriculum on reservations, thus affecting the content offered.

Image Distortion and Stereotypes

The inaccurate portrayal of Indigenous peoples in our educational system and in Hollywood are at the root of the misunderstanding and denigration of the original people of this land. As author Jennifer Raff wrote, "Histories of the Americas written by non-Native scholars tend to be dominated by the story of how Europeans colonized the continents. In some cases, academics repackage and re-interpret traditional knowledge as their own scholarship without credit to Native experts" (2022, xix-xx).

John Wayne and Hollywood played a significant role in distorting the image of Native America. Hollywood and "historic" novels sensationalized warfare and the warrior, focusing on Plains Indians and the Apaches to the exclusion of all others. That emphasis on war and aggression comes out of the mentality of an invading people, not a people in defense of their homeland. This John Wayne quote embodies the rationalization of white supremacy over Indigenous peoples: "Our so-called stealing of this country from them [Native Americans] was just a matter of survival. There were substantial numbers of people who needed new land, and the Indians were selfishly trying to keep it for themselves."

Hollywood movies, novels, and a flawed educational system have created an exaggerated and inaccurate view of Indigenous peoples.

Most Americans imagine all Indigenous peoples living in tipis, which in fact were only used by some of the Great Plains peoples. Even in that area there were other forms of housing, such as large earth lodges used by the Pawnee, Mandan, Hidatsa, and Arikara. The Wichita (Kitikiti'sh) and other Caddoan peoples further south built large lodges made of poles and thick prairie grasses. The sedentary tribal plains economy was based on agriculture (growing corn, beans, and squash) along with hunting, fishing, and gathering.

The Great Plains were home to many original peoples and also migrations from the eastern regions, which intensified due to the Euro-American invasion in the 17th and 18th century.

Another misunderstanding of Indigenous culture is the ignorance surrounding the many status relationships in which Native men and women served their communities.

The Indigenous meaning of warrior is much broader than the English meaning. In the native sense, it can relate to one who faces and overcomes her/his own fears and is courageous and self-disciplined. With that broader view, the concept crosses gender lines. Tatanka Iyotake (Sitting Bull) explained it this way:

> Warriors are not what you think of as warriors. The warrior is not someone who fights, because no one has the right to take another life. The warrior, for us, is one who sacrifices himself for the good of others. His task is to take care of the elderly, the defenseless, those who cannot provide for themselves, and above all, the children, the future of humanity.

After tribal members had engaged in a conflict, the Lakota, as an example, had re-entry ceremonies so each individual could return to the status and behavior of a community member. This involved the purification of weapons and smudging, along with ceremonial songs, before reentering the community. Relatives would welcome loved ones at the edge of the village after the ceremonial songs were complete. This process provided a transition from conflict back to membership in the family and community. I find this practice extraordinarily relevant when considering today's world.

Our current society could learn something from this Indigenous process. This ritual of re-entry reduced possible post-traumatic stress syndrome. The transition from a situation of extreme stress to the calm of tribal life helped mitigate the effects of conflict-derived stress on the community.

As environmental impacts, the spread of Euro-American diseases, and attacks by the U.S. military intensified, many of these healthy cultural practices were modified or abandoned in a desperate attempt to adjust to rapidly changing conditions.

Hollywood has denigrated native peoples with stereotypes like "whooping war calls" as natives attacked "innocent" white people. I have personally experienced that slapping the mouth response when people find out about my interest in Native America. It puts me in an awkward position, but I try to correct that image when that embarrassing opportunity arises—the reality of the Indigenous "warrior" is so different from the stereotype perpetuated by Euro-American culture.

In Indigenous ethos, women create trilling sounds to reflect community unification and support courageous action. They provide an emotional connection within the community. And they come out of a psyche that never says goodbye. In Lakota, one might say *tókša akhe*, which roughly translates into, "Until we meet again." It is difficult to translate Indigenous languages word for word due to the cultural differences in processing language—it is easier to translate the meanings. The above translation does just that, alluding to the understanding that in life and death, we are always together as one.

The feminine role has four foundational values. The Lakota terms for those are: *wowahokunkiya* (lead) *wokage* (create), *nakicizin* (protect), and *wachantognaka* (nurture). As in male roles, there are overlapping values that function somewhat differently *relative to* gender. It is also important to remember that Indigenous roles are not rigid; rather, they flow more freely. For example, if a woman feels best in a masculine role, she is not pressured to be "feminine" as in some Euro-American societies.

These are all characteristics of Native American tribal life. I am using Lakota/Dakota/Nakota examples because that is what I am most familiar with through my adopted relatives from that tribal culture, but it applies to North American tribes across the country.

Using the Past to Find a Better Future

It is interesting to study conflicting thought patterns in U.S. policy toward the original peoples of this land. Often, we find recognition merging with rationalization.

One example is New York attorney Felix Cohen's (1907–1953) *Handbook of Federal Indian Law*, in which he wrote, "It is out of a rich Indian democratic tradition that the distinctive political ideals of American life emerged."

The book compiled expert thinking in Indigenous law and provided a vast overview of Native America that caused considerable friction between Cohen and his supervisors. It's not clear what the Justice Department's motivations were. What is obvious is that the handbook justified the existence of the U.S. and its history relative to Indigenous America. At the same time, according to the Justice Department, it also gave too much power to the tribes.

A Clearer Vision of Tribalism

There can be no honest progress in the scientific study of the past without acknowledging those threads of human history we have dismissed, neglected, or erased. The journey to knowledge has to involve self-scrutiny; scientific progress cannot be divorced from the social context in which it takes place.

Jennifer Raff, *Origin: A Genetic History of the Americas*

We have to get honest about the traditional Native cultures.

Indigenous peoples cannot be categorized into neat boxes and binary dichotomies. They viewed the world holistically, seeing events as part of a flowing pattern of relativity and addressing issues in realistic terms. Their process unified feminine foresight and masculine practical action. There was no absolute authority in tribalism. Political decisions were grounded in clan authority, often led by the Elder clan mothers. The child-nurturing process enabled individuals to make independent decisions, and at the same time, led to a unified community as opposed to materialistic, egotistical self-interest. That nurturing process and community relationships that included the natural world made it unnecessary to use laws, force, or threat in maintaining order. Indigenous ethos was more effective and sustainable.

The ethos of tribalism contains solutions to our current problems of polarization, delusional attitudes, and alienation. Disasters like the storming of the Capitol on January 6, 2021, the riots across the country, the attempted assassination of Donald Trump, and other acts of violence reflecting socio-political alienation are clear warning signs of intensifying danger.

It is impossible to ignore that nation-state socio-political patterns pose serious problems.

Colonists and authors who took their information from colonial writings, did not, and still do not, understand traditional Indigenous governance. They tended to see the Indigenous sachems or chiefs as authority figures, projecting their own Euro-American processes onto Indigenous cultures.

One practice that blinded them to the reality of Indigenous leadership was that chiefs' positions could be inherited, like the monarchies in Europe. But the similarities end there. Indigenous leadership played the role of facilitator more than authority figure. For example, in the *Tsenacommacah* Confederacy in what is now Virginia, the *Powhatan* did not have absolute authority. The *quiakros* (clan Elders) served as advisers and had the power to override any decision the *Powhatan* made. The *quiakros* emerged from clan consensus building, which influenced the decisions of local independent communities. This helps explain the relatively slow response from the *Tsenacommacah* Confederacy to atrocities committed by the Virginia Colony, something the tribes had not experienced before the arrival of Europeans.

The following chapters describe a value system that mitigated problems caused by materialistic nation-state forms of organization and offer better ideas for approaching the challenges we face today.

> *Treat the earth well: it was not given to you by your parents, it was loaned to you by your children. We do not inherit the earth from our Ancestors, we borrow it from our children.*
>
> —TaSunka Witko (Crazy Horse)

CHAPTER 3

THE CRITICAL ROLE OF LANGUAGE

In connecting language, culture, and knowledge, Anne Waters, as quoted in Margaret Kovach's book *Indigenous Methodologies*, suggested that "dualistic constructs such as like/unlike have resulted in a binary language and thought pattern in European cultures. Conversely, in Indigenous cultures the language constructs suggest a non-binary, complementary philosophy of the world" (2009, 72).

Put another way, Bibiana Ancheta (Tulalip/Coastal Salish) explained, "Identity comes from our culture, our culture comes from our language, and our language comes from our environment"(Wilbur, 2023, 65).

Noam Chomsky, MIT Professor of Linguistics Emeritus, seems to align with Waters and Ancheta in his view about the way language determines how one sees the world. He pointed out that "the structure of language determines not only thought, but reality itself."

This is why understanding Native American languages is essential to understanding Native American thought and identity.

The relational aspect of Indigenous language centers on relativity as opposed to the binary either/or mentality. That, in part, explains the early peaceful response of Indigenous peoples to the European presence. The mind that sees in inclusive terms responds from a sense of relationship, while the binary linguistic process focuses on identifying differences. And that, in part, illustrates how the European focus was on difference and objectification as opposed to similarities.

A profound example is found in European Christianity where "evil" is represented by an Anti-Christ, antithetical to the Christ. This reflects a mentality that thinks in oppositional terms. At Jamestown as well as the Caribbean, the European oppositional mindset interfaced with an Indigenous inclusive thought process. Out of that inclusivity arises a language and mentality that views nature in terms of sustainability and relationships as a balance rather than as opposition. The Indigenous way of seeing the natural world as equal partners in sustainability is reflected in Indigenous languages.

Similarly, in tribal societies, relationships were a defining value, and interpersonal relationships were expressed linguistically. Native Americans referred to each other by relational status, such as uncle and brother. And those were further defined. A Lakota man's older brother was called Chiye, Misun was younger brother, and Mitankala younger sister, etc. Interactions would flow differently based on the relational status of those involved. The behavior around a mother-in-law was clearly defined in ways of proper respect. With a foundation of connection, language and conversation were not adversarial, more focused on "we" than "I."

They had individual names, but the names were spiritual in nature and mostly used in spiritual contexts.

The deep value of relationships was reflected in how they treated each other and their universe. This is why, in tribal societies, wealth was measured by sharing as opposed to personal accumulation. One did not own land or much individual property, and though territories were recognized, borders were not formed.

Through language, Native American tribalism wove together subtle interpersonal interactions, ecological relationships, childhood nurturing, consensus-building governance, feminine/masculine equality, and tribal clan organizational structures. These governed their inter- and intra-tribal relationships and spirituality. Indigenous language created a consciousness that perceived an interrelationship with the whole, each individual being inseparable from that oneness. The "self" was seen as part of a universal flow of energy, much like autumn leaves turn beautiful colors, fall to the ground, and enrich the soil of Mother Earth to complete the circle of life.

It is difficult to accurately talk about one aspect of Indigenous culture without including the others. The Euro-American linear-binary linguistic perspective misses the entire interplay between those conventions. This was the culture that met the colonists. And, in spite of all that has happened, that culture still exists within Indigenous languages and among traditional native peoples.

Object vs. Concept

In her book *Indigenous Methodologies*, Margaret Kovach, Canadian Nehiyaw (Cree) scholar and university professor, wrote,

"*Kiskeyihtâmowin* [Nehiyaw Cree for epistemology] includes beliefs held about knowledge, where it comes from and whom it involves." She added that those who attempt "to fit Indigenous epistemologies into Western cultural conceptual rubrics expressed through the English language are destined to feel the squirm." That "squirm" is due to the vast linguistic differences between cultures deeply grounded in a spiritual relationship with the natural world and those that are not.

Our entertainment industry provides countless examples of narratives interwoven with objectification rather than oneness. Fictionalized characters are often engaged in solving crimes of violence or accomplishing personal feats, capitalizing on the sensational, as opposed to interactive narratives portraying sensitive, caring relationships.

In the more holistic and relational Indigenous thought process, words are generally combinations of stand-alone words/syllables. When combining them into a single relationship, a unique meaning emerges. For example, the Lakota word for woman is *winyan,* made up of two stand-alone words/syllables: *Wi*, meaning sun, and *inyan,* meaning earth or stone. When merged, these create the word "woman." In the native thought process, the unification of energy from the sun and earth causes sustainability through the birth of everything organic. Women, by giving birth, sustain our communities. Hence the unification of Mother Earth and Father Sun, the feminine and the masculine, creating the foundation of an egalitarian culture. This illustrates how Indigenous languages promote thinking in a flow of relational oneness.

Native American metaphor, discussed in detail in Chapters 6 and 7, evolved from stand-alone words/syllables being united to form deeper relational meanings. This use of language creates a unification between concepts that builds into a relationship, while European languages rely on linear-binary categories that often leads to over-categorization and stereotyping. European languages miss the subtlety of metaphorical meanings in lengthy narratives. If one's first language is of European origin, those linear-binary tendencies are only mitigated through familiarity.

Linguistic differences likely influenced the relationships and conflicts between the Euro-Americans and the Lakota, Cheyenne, and Arapahoe peoples in 1876. The U.S. Government had negotiated reservation boundaries and hunting territories in the Treaty of 1868. However, for Indigenous peoples, boundaries were understood in relation to nature, such as the migratory patterns of the buffalo. This difference in perspective heightened tensions over the use of the Black Hills for hunting, and worsened when the Northern Pacific Railroad proposed installing tracks through Lakota land. All of this led to the U.S. sending three military units to trap the Native peoples, in what was seen as a violation of artificially drawn boundary lines. Battles ensued with both General Crook at the Battle of the Rosebud and, eight days later, Lt. Col. Custer at Greasy Grass (Little Big Horn).

This is a good example of how understanding linguistic differences can change our perception of intercultural interactions and responses.

Common examples of Euro-American metaphors are "beat a dead horse," "couch potato," etc., with more complex metaphoric examples mostly existing in poetry. But, compared to the thousands of lengthy and ancient Indigenous narratives made up of standalone words combined to create and reference complex multiple meanings, Euro-American metaphors tend to be shorter and less complex. For example, compare "couch potato" to *gizhewaadizi*, at the root of the Anishinaabe *Indinawemaaganidog* (All My Relatives), which reflects how Native cultures are grounded in values of giving, respect, kindness, and generosity that encompasses the vegetation, animals, stars, and all that exists in the universe. The importance of that relationship between all things is reflected in their word/phrase *wenji-bimaad-iziyaang*, meaning "from what, or where, we get our living, our life." Human behavior is expressed in Anishinaabe as *Gwayahkooshkawin*, meaning life in balance; to conduct one's life in the middle ground where harmony is achieved. In Lakota, that is captured in the word *wolakota*, meaning living with good hearts and minds. It is a way of being rather than a way of doing. That Indigenous perspective sees in terms of coming together in peace, balance, and harmony in the circle of life in which all is connected in relationship.

Words like the Ojibwe *Indinawemaaganidog* and the Lakota *Mitakuye Oyasin* (both meaning All My Relatives), summarize the deep interconnection and meaning of "relationship." Brenda Child, in her book *Holding Our World Together*, explains Indigenous perspective like this: "In the Ojibwe worldview, the natural world and cultural formations such as music and dance coexist in a symbiotic partnership that is essential to the good life. ...Generosity was a highly developed value on the spiritual road to a good life and was ritualized in ceremony and diplomacy" (2010, 92).

This is why the arriving Europeans saw a pristine environment grounded in sustainability.

Words like the Anishinaabe *Indinawemaaganidog* and the

Lakota *Wolakota* go a long way in explaining why first contact with Europeans was peaceful.

If your first language is Indigenous, there is no disconnect from nature, no "rising above" it. Everything has a spirit, including the stones that make up Mother Earth.

Understanding Indigenous languages is imperative to understanding the Native thought process and philosophy of relationships, including the historical responses to the invasion of their homeland. Failure to understand the Native thought process opened the door to Euro-American projection and bias toward vastly different cultures.

For example, *Tipi* is the Lakota word that identifies the space within a circle which is home, a place where loved ones live in relationship. In contrast, non-Indigenous language encourages the mind to see the tipi as an object. Indigenous languages are more focused on the space within, where close relationships with family and friends occur. In other words, Indigenous languages reflect a perspective focused on relationships as opposed to objectification. This significant linguistic difference changes how the mind sees and interprets reality. The cultural difference is profound. It explains why individual property was less valued than interpersonal relationships. To give a parallel, it is the difference between a house (a structure) and a home (the place where sustenance, rest and caring relationships occur).

Another example: *Hocokah,* a Lakota word often translated as circle, really means the space captured within, where all relationships occur. Everything within *Hocokah* manifests a spiritual reality.

In binary languages, I have heard lectures that suggest the

Anishinaabe denigrated the Dakota by calling them "snakes." This misses the vastly different thought process of Indigenous peoples. The word snake does not have the negative connotation to Indigenous peoples that it has to Euro-Americans. Native peoples have this sense, as cultural historian Richard Tarnas stated, of "undifferentiated participatory" inclusivity. The Anishinaabe word *natowessiwak* more accurately means "those who speak a different language or have different ways." The key part of the Ojibwa psyche here is the concept of "different." The word *natowessiwak* in ancient times represented snake as different anatomically from others in the same category. In the case of a nearby people, it implies an environmental and cultural difference. Indigenous people often referenced neighboring people relative to their environmental surroundings, not as enemies or inferiors as was the tendency of Euro-Americans. Non-native translations believed that by calling Dakota people "snakes," Ojibwa people were denigrating them, projecting Euro-American attitudes toward snakes on a culture with very different perspectives.

In Anishinaabe, *giinebig* is a generalized term for snake, not *natowessiwak,* but variants exist in local dialects. Different regions use different words when speaking in context. *Ndaawaabiigtaa* in eastern Ojibwa and Odawa means "to twist and move its body around." There are specific words for different kinds of snakes, for example, *zhiishiigwe* (rattlesnake), or *newe* (bull snake). In this case, the different nouns for snake were often more expository, reducing the tendency of the mind to objectify and increasing the sense of relationship.

These distinctions are critical because, as Waters stated above, "form gives rise to a way of thinking and being." In the case of specific Indigenous words, context is important in understanding their broader meaning, especially in *relationship,* as opposed to the more linear-binary European languages, which tend to lack that fluidity of meaning in context and tend to see in terms of objects as opposed to relationships. It is a major difference between object-oriented and relationship-oriented cultures. Stand-alone words merging to form a broader conceptual meaning causes the mind to understand the depth of that oneness in motion, that unification of all that is.

It is easy to assume that all tribes were alike, but this is incorrect. Each had its own traditions. For example, before Euro-American expansion created territorial pressures between tribes and introduced European diseases, the Dakota Sioux and Ojibwa were frequent trading partners. There were likely rare cases of inter-tribal marriage, despite the Dakota reckoning kinship matrilineally and the Anishinaabe being patrilineal.

As Matthew Wildcat (Nehiyaw Plains Cree; PhD in Political Science, University of British Columbia; Political Science and Native Studies Professor at the University of Alberta) wrote, the same principle of kinship and relation is expressed in the *Nehiyaw* (Cree) language as *Wahkohtowin.* The *Nehiyaw* concept reflects a worldview in which all living beings (trees, animals, humans, stars) are relatives. As mentioned above, in the Anishinaabe language the same principle is encapsulated in *Indinawemaaganidog.* In Lakota, it is *Mitakuye Oyasin* (All My Relatives). All three reflect the broader Indigenous definition of community and the Native value of cooperative relationship between tribes and the natural world. That is why Native languages tend to put more focus on the outcomes of actions which, over time, provided for greater sustainability and less aggressive behavior against other peoples. Hence, the initial peaceful Tsenacommacah response to the settlement of Jamestown and the Virginia Colony.

Linguistic Misunderstandings

Much mythmaking about Indigenous people has arisen from misunderstandings of the intricacies of native languages. As Noam Chomsky expressed, we learn to perceive and understand the world through our first language, making it important to gain an appreciation for the cultural differences reflected in Indigenous language.

Some Euro-American authors projected their own mentality onto Native cultures, neatly categorizing them, perhaps for psychological comfort, while distorting reality. Two more examples, one Iroquois and one Lakota, illustrate the fundamental differences between Indigenous peoples and those who sought to study them.

First, there is the misuse of the word "woman," projecting Euro-American status-relationships on egalitarian cultures.

Euro-American authors often try to prove that the Iroquois disrespected the Lenni Lenapi people by calling them "women." This is a projection of sexist Euro-American attitudes onto an egalitarian Iroquois mentality. It also reflects the European linguistic focus on differences as opposed to commonalities.

In Indigenous societies, women were considered the foundation of the culture and of cultural identity—the feminine side of our humanity that reflects wisdom. When the Iroquois referred to the Lenni Lenapi as "women," they were honoring them as people of spiritual wisdom. In Native societies, feminine and masculine values existed in harmony.

In European languages, nouns are usually one word. In contrast, Indigenous languages tend to use descriptions in place of nouns, describing the characteristics associated with that entity and the interacting relationships between them.

An example is the Lakota word *unshimila*, which roughly translates to mean "concern for the well-being and needs of the world community." The Jesuits translated it to mean "I am pitiful," with the narrow focus on an egotistical sense of personal need or neediness. The Euro-American focus sees ego while the Indigenous mind moves more in rhythmic consciousness of the whole.

This is why ethnographic accuracy is critical in understanding cultural beliefs, attitudes, and responses. History written to justify conquest, or written out of ignorance or egotistical imperatives, distorts reality.

Understanding Differences in Language Is Essential

> *If a person is able to speak Cherokee, they see a whole new concept, ideology, world view that doesn't exist in a white man's world, in a white man's English. ... That's the genesis of who we are, the essence of who we are, the language.* (Wilbur, 2023, 130)
>
> —Harry Oosahwee, Cherokee

North American Indigenous languages differ so greatly from Euro-American languages that, during World Wars I and II, the U.S. military employed Indigenous speakers from various tribes as "code talkers." In WWI, Choctaw was the most used to confuse the opposition, but others, including Cheyenne, Cherokee, Comanche, Ho-Chunk/Winnebago, Osage, and Yankton Dakota Sioux also served.

In WWII, Navajo, Assiniboine, Cherokee, Cheyenne, Chippewa, Choctaw, Comanche, Cree, Crow, Hopi, Kiowa, Menominee, Sauk, Meskwaki, Mississauga, Muscogee, Osage, Pawnee, Seminole, and Sioux served in both Europe and the Pacific as code talkers. The Navajo code talkers served mostly in the Pacific. Some strategists believe the war could not have been won without the code talkers, because none of the opposing militaries could break the code, not even the linguists of Japan. This is extraordinary considering the efforts by boarding schools in the U.S. and Canada to destroy Native languages by severely punishing children caught speaking in their native tongue.

It is difficult for non-native speakers to fully grasp the meanings of Indigenous words, as subtle nuances can change the interpretation. For example, the conflation of the word "warrior" with "American Indian" is a Euro-American linguistic projection: In the Euro-American mind, "Indian" is almost synonymous with "warrior," a fighter in warbonnet. But that conflation misunderstands the sophisticated native cultures. The Lakota word *Akicita* is often translated as "warrior," but an exact translation into English, which settles for a rough approximation, misses the nuance of meaning. It more accurately translates to "message," meaning the *Akicita* see that order is maintained in the community through messaging or communication. Related to warrior or *Akicita* is the word *Woohetike*, meaning bravery, or courage. Both words encompass much more than what is meant by the English term "warrior."

"Warrior" defines a status relationship that, in Native languages, relates more to serving the community courageously, sometimes in the face of danger. It is not as specific or violent as in Euro-American languages; rather it is only one of the roles an individual may have in service to family and community.

Every clan and tribe had its own identity and culture, but there were important similarities. Despite vastly different environmental conditions and cultures across the continent, an examination of the Indigenous language families—such as Siouan, Algonquin, Uto-Aztecan, Athabascan—reveals similar patterns in structure, mental processes, and interpretation. This similarity is grounded in relationship to all that is, which explains why initial Indigenous contact with Europeans was peaceful.

Language: The Value of Balance

Understanding Indigenous languages conceptually is essential to grasping the Indigenous principles of sustainability. While Native peoples made changes to their environment, they did not disrupt the sustainability of each species or the natural balance. In contrast, colonists made destructive alterations to the environment, which led to eventual climate change.

The Indigenous sense of being in relationship with the world around them was overlooked by the Euro-American materialistic mindset. That sense of relationship also explains why Indigenous cultural development did not mirror European materialism but was instead grounded in environmental relationships.

All life emanates from the union of Mother Earth and Father Sun, and this understanding placed the linguistic focus on relationships, not objects. This was the foundation of intra- and intertribal cooperation and explains why the Indigenous psyche sought unification as opposed to difference, inclusivity as opposed to exclusivity. For example, the Lakota word *tiwahe* can easily be translated into English as "family." But it is more layered than that. It also refers to a complete interconnectedness between all that is living, emphasizing the importance of taking responsibility for the well-being of family, community, and environment. The speaker's meaning in the use of *tiwahe* becomes clear in the context of the sentence, but it also always implies the broader meaning.

The loss of Indigenous language has been disastrous for Native peoples. Dr. Jessica Metcalfe, of the Turtle Mountain Chippewa, describes the profound mental and physical trauma caused by Euro-American "education." She states, "You must know your language, because sometimes the assimilation assault was so strong. People who we need to teach us how to pronounce words have had such a traumatic experience with boarding schools that they do not want to speak their language; they literally had it beaten out of them" (Wilbur, 2010, 51).

Given the high rate of Indigenous teen suicide, providing native youth with the opportunity to see life through their ancestorial language could very well save lives.

Learning ways of thinking beyond Euro-American materialism

broadens our understanding of human potential and may help us find solutions to the problems our country faces today.

> For Indigenous peoples, overcoming the trauma of the past is critical. Indigenous language offers a pathway to healthy recovery—physically, emotionally, psychologically, spiritually, and culturally. Jocelyn Jones, of the *Onoñda'gegá* (People of the Great Hills), highlights the healing properties of language: "By being able to create more speakers, and teach culture, ceremony, a lifeway, and values of our people, we could see a lot of abuse cycles all through Indigenous Country resolve themselves" (Wilbur, 2010, 80).

CHAPTER 4

ESSENTIAL VALUES OF AMERICAN TRIBALISM

Before our white brothers came to civilize us, we had no jails. Therefore, we had no criminals. We had no locks or keys, and so we had no thieves. If a man was so poor that he had no horse, tipi or blanket, someone gave him these things. We were too uncivilized to set much value on personal belongings. We wanted to have things only in order to give them away. We had no money, and therefore a man's worth couldn't be measured by it.

—Mniconwoju, Lakota Chief John Fire Lame Deer

Indigenous societies were organized through a democratic, bottom-up decision-making process that emanated from lineages. It was through the lineage system that feminine/masculine balance and discipline were sustained. Elders in the lineage offered wise leadership and proper restraint. That is why no police, jails, prisons, or standing armies were necessary in Indigenous societies anywhere in North America. The land was held by the community, not by individuals. And that community was made up of all that lives: humans, plants, and animals, along with spiritual forces.

The cultural ethos emphasized egalitarianism in the relationship between local clans and their chosen leaders in maintaining social order. Oratory was a highly developed skill, and in many cases, diplomacy mitigated the use of force.

The Indigenous Mind

What it means to be Indigenous is best expressed by Indigenous people themselves.

In his book *The Man Made of Words*, Kiowa poet, author, and professor N. Scott Momaday illustrates the subtlety of Indigenous thought through a story his father told him when he was growing up.

The story is about a woman who was buried in a cabinet wearing a beautiful buckskin dress embellished with beads and elk's teeth. While the location has been lost, you can look to the east of his grandfather Mammedaty's home to see its general location. And that is remembered and passed on by each generation. The woman's name is unknown.

It's a simple story. Or is it? What is the meaning of the metaphors? It undoubtedly varies from listener to listener. Momaday wrote: "That the concentration of things that are explicitly remembered—the general landscape, the simple, almost abstract nature of the burial, above all the beautiful dress, which is wholly singular (in kind as well as in its function within the narrative)—is especially Indian in character."

Momaday acknowledges the physical qualities of the grave and what is in it. He also sees beyond the concrete. His description of the burial and the dress reflects whole brain understanding. The linear-binary thought process does not interpret but instead focuses on a story about a woman buried in a dress. The Indigenous perspective sees the metaphor and meaning of the story, each person finding meanings for themselves. For example, what is the meaning of the woman and the fact the dress is beautiful? Is it a metaphor for the land? Why are the elk and the land important? What is the relationship between the burial and Momaday's view of the land? Is it a story about the woman, or our relationship to the land, or the design on the dress and the elk teeth? This is clearly more than just a story about an unnamed person buried "out there."

The Indigenous and Euro-American thought processes differ greatly. The relationship-oriented Indigenous people saw the world as one body, where "we" included all of nature—all of *Maka Ina na Unci Maka*, the Lakota words for Mother and Grandmother Earth.

From this Indigenous perspective emerged the value of humans existing in sustainable balance with their environment. Given the fact that natural resources are finite, a more far-sighted industrial approach, along with a more communitarian focus, interfaced with Washington leadership, may be at least a manageable initial approach to environmental issues.

Sustainability

Thomas Banyacya Sr., a Hopi spokesperson for the Elders, first warned humanity of approaching environmental disaster in the

1940s, while the Euro-American world has spent the past decades catching up.

Film star Richard Gere narrated a documentary titled *The Earth is Warming the Earth,* which explores feedback loops. The introduction of the documentary includes comments by the Dalai Lama and Swedish environmental activist Greta Thunberg.

The introduction to the film states: "Fossil fuel emissions … have … set in motion nature's own feedback loops, which are raising temperatures even higher. The urgent question is: Are we approaching a point of no return, leading to an uninhabitable Earth, or do we have the vision and will to slow, halt, and reverse them?"

The documentary highlights a fundamental value in traditional Native American societies: sustainability. At the core of that issue is the definition of power. Many cultural layers supported Indigenous sustainability, and the spiritual definition of power was a critical layer. Intertwined with this spiritual definition was an egalitarian socio-political system that embraced both gender equality and a harmonious relationship with the natural world.

> *Humans are not capable of power.*
> *Only the Spirit has power.*
> *Humans are capable of strength.*
> *The source of human strength is gentleness.*
> —Leon Shenandoah,
> Chief of the Six Nations Grand Council

The European invasion of the western hemisphere brought a completely different definition of power (discussed in Chapter 1):

materialism that included influence, leverage, force, and material wealth. The issues exposed in the documentary on environmental feedback loops stem from that shift in definition. This shift is at the root of our current environmental issues today and poses a significant threat to sustainability.

The predominant American linear-binary thought process has yet to incorporate the layers of thought found in Indigenous cultures. The Indigenous definition of power as spiritual was critical to environmental health and foundational to the concept of sustainability. That thought process is "whole brain," metaphorically seeing both the forest and the canopy at the same time.

Indigenous Critical Thinking Process

As a high school educator, I taught my students a critical thinking process that involved identifying and analyzing a problem through hypothesis development, researching and finding relevant facts to assess that hypothesis, and drawing conclusions. The final step was to develop generalizations that explain human behavior under specific circumstances.

Ancient Indigenous peoples applied the same process to understand how the natural world operates. I once attended a symposium conducted by a traditional basket maker. I was fascinated by how her mind worked. She used three different plants to weave her baskets. Her first challenge was determining when each plant could be gathered based on the exact amount of moisture contained in the plant. The optimal window lasts only about two weeks out of a year, and each plant has its own maturation timing. Another variable is that no two harvest years are identical. She had to determine the perfect time to harvest each of the three different plants based on her observations of the weather each year. They had to be stored in soil containing the right amount of moisture until she was ready to prepare them for weaving.

The same was true with hunting and calculating variables in migration patterns and weather. Indigenous critical thinking was at the core of Native relationships and their understanding of the oneness of motion in the universe. In ancient times, Hopi farmers knew exactly when to plant the first seed by observing the motion of the sun and watching the slight variations of weather patterns.

Child nurturing was also grounded in critical thinking and analysis. People who lived close to the land and the rhythms of nature learned critical thinking skills as children growing into adulthood and how to work in oneness with the entire community.

Communication Through Body Language

Tribal linguistics represent only a portion of communication. There is also a distinct tribal body language which is difficult to explain but easy to experience. Over my forty years of personal relationships with traditional peoples, I experienced a distinct ethos learned through body language. I became aware of it through their responses to something I was doing that was considered inappropriate by tribal standards.

My first experience occurred years ago, when I was handling a pipe used in spiritual communication called a *canumpa* (pronounced "cha-num'-pa"), translating roughly to "the mating of the feminine with the masculine." A young man, probably half my age, conveyed unmistakable body language that clearly outlined the proper and respectful way to handle a *canumpa*. He said nothing, not even looking at me, but it was a clear signal that I was not handling the pipe properly. I can recall two other times when body language told me I was responding inappropriately relative to the relationship: one from a man and one a from woman.

Those three expressions I will never forget. The lines of propriety were clear without a word being said. I learned on those three occasions something subtle about the meaning of relationships and communication within tribalism. This language is gentler than the spoken word, and unforgettable. There are subtleties in relationship-oriented tribal behavior that people from more aggressive, materialistic societies can easily miss. And yet, it is human to be gentle. We are conditioned to be harsh and aggressive.

> *Nothing is so*
> *Strong as*
> *Gentleness, nothing so gentle as real*
> *Strength.*
> —Saint Francis de Sales

The Wisdom of the Elders

To better understand Indigenous communities, one must understand their thought process, which often included metaphor and relationship. It was the valued tribal Elders and their wisdom that fostered foresight and served as the foundation for community well-being and sustainability. Elders taught respect through example in all their relationships with the natural world. The cultivation of that respect assured long-term well-being by nurturing children with knowledge. Tribal Elders provided that guiding light for the children and the community, and they were treated with utmost respect by all age groups. It was the Elders that stabilized and solidified the Indigenous heart and soul.

Inclusivity and Acceptance

As historian Eve Ball wrote in her book *Indeh: An Apache Odyssey*, "Native America often lauded unique individuals, perceiving them as special/blessed, rather than ostracizing them." This was certainly true of Lozen, who at an early age demonstrated all the skills attributed to warriors as well as being a brilliant military strategist.

There are many heroic Indigenous women in history whose stories have been lost. Fortunately, Lozen's has not.

The Indigenous inhabitants of North America, unlike Europeans, were far more likely to *celebrate* differences. Lozen (Dexterous Horse Thief) was a "two spirit" whose constant companion was her female partner, Dahteste. She was also a heroic warrior, prognosticator, and gifted medicine woman with vast herbal knowledge.

Lozen's spirit was of the homeland, of the rising sun, of *Ussen*, the Apache name for the Creator. Her spiritual powers included the ability to reach beyond her five senses and "see" American and Mexican troop movements from great distances and into the future. She played a prominent role in success against both the American and Mexican armies. She eventually joined Geronimo, with whom she shared her abilities, making him even more elusive than before.

Lozen believed her powers were given to her by the Creator to protect her people, so she rode with the warriors. One of her accomplishments occurred when a large American army unit was approaching, forcing the Apaches to attempt to cross a flooding river with their children and women. The warriors hesitated, but Lozen challenged the raging waters on horseback, making several trips as she took each child to safety. The rest crossed without a loss following her display of courage.

Native Democracy: A Model Based on Relationship and Consensus

Native American communities have an organizational process that flows from the grassroots to a comprehensive movement, which is vastly different from nation-state thinking and its hierarchical power structure.

Today, despite major disruption to the Indigenous organizational process, you can still see elements of it in both Native spirituality and powwows. They act without the hierarchy so common in Euro-American organizational structures. You see it manifesting in the timing of everything. This is why non-Indigenous people sometimes see disorder where there is actually highly sophisticated order that moves with the motion of the universe.

What often eludes non-Native consciousness is the issue of rhythmic time, and it is that rhythm that organizes Indigenous action. It is also why diverse and independent tribal cultures could act in unison against the British during the French and Indian War.

Timing Is Part of Native Governance

There are jokes about "Indian time," but the fact is, Newtonian interval time is not in rhythm with the natural world. Native time is. To be Indigenous is to be unified with that rhythm, and also, in ironic contrast to Newton's interval time, with the laws of physics.

There is an Indigenous cultural ethos which unifies tribal action with the motion of nature's rhythms and shapes Indigenous democracies. It is why non-Native people sometimes arrive at a powwow right on time or early only to find that the drummers, who start the program, have not yet arrived. British quantum physicist F. David Peat theorized that Indigenous spirituality might open some doors for his research. He flew into British Columbia to attend a Native Sundance, arriving "on time" only to find nothing was happening. That experience started him on a journey which eventually led to his book *Blackfoot Physics*.

Forty years ago, when I started attending Lakota and Dakota ceremonies, I witnessed leadership without a hierarchy. It was not immediately apparent, but the influence of Elders was critical: in the shadows, but ever-present.

I will never forget going on my first *hamblecia* (vision quest) under the leadership of Leonard Crowdog. It was clear during the experience that "leadership" in that world was more about the universe and its spiritual forces than about the individual. Crowdog's gentle humility in that spiritual context is hard to capture in the written word, yet it embodied what leadership means in the Indigenous world. It was grounded more in wisdom and personal and care than authority or hierarchy.

Being in Community

Crowdog's mother, an Elder, came up to me after the Inipi ceremony that reintroduced me into society after I came down from the "vision quest." She shook my hand and thanked me for my gift of sacrifice for the community. I will never forget the feeling—the gift of humble connection to community—in that moment.

To have a respected Elder express appreciation gave me a deep sense as part of that oneness which can only be felt, not explained. That connection translates into a sense of togetherness, of caring about community.

That togetherness is the foundation of Indigenous democracy. It explains why, during tribal emergencies, each clan member could make personal decisions that differed from the group's and remain respected. It is why a hierarchical structure was unnecessary. That unforgettable wisdom emanating from the Elders, combined with nurturing relationships into adulthood, was the glue of community. Each member could act in unison without indoctrination. It also explains why individuals making choices in opposition to the clan was extremely rare. Paradoxically, that sense of individuality that emerged out of nurturance was the very source of tribal community in unified action. It put the "unity" in community.

Interestingly, that flow of energy also created a form of sustainability through productive diversity in agriculture. One might see these as separate topics, but in the Indigenous reality, agricultural diversity and consensus-building democracies are connected. Spirituality, agriculture, and governance dance together. The Indigenous perspective views community as the interconnectedness of all that is inorganic and organic.

In Chapter 6, I discuss some deeper meanings of Native design—a design philosophy that is not about "art," but about metaphor. Gaining insight into the metaphorical meanings in that design philosophy is foundational for understanding Indigenous consensus-building democracies.

This is because Indigenous "art" reflects the thought process of unity between all things. The aspects of Indigenous culture cannot be understood separately; all parts of their culture move together in complete unification and harmony as one.

Today, despite the cultural disruptions caused by the Euro-American invasion, we can still see Indigenous organizational structure in that flow during powwows. There is no visible hierarchy, but spiritual energy moves through subtle leadership.

Indigenous democracies emanated out of the clan structure, a bottom-up decision-making process in which each clan member had a voice—each family member listened to the other without interruption. It is this subtle but effective organizational structure which gave each tribal member a level of personal liberty that was so clearly described in the writings of Roger Williams in early colonial times. The source of that liberty is also the source of unified action, as well as the source of compassionate decision-making.

A Different Definition of War

Conflicts with Europeans forced Indigenous peoples to adjust their definition of war, as their survival was at stake. Before colonization, warfare was limited to raids involving perhaps a few warriors, but certainly not massive armies. Anthropologist Paul Radin, who devoted much of his career to the study of the Winnebago and Anishinaabeg peoples, captured the meaning of warrior and the relationship to community:

> An individual might go on the warpath either alone or in company with a few people, but the community, in the person of the chief, insisted that he show

> some warrant for his action. If no warrant of any kind could be given, he subjected himself to the only restrictive measures the chief and the community could adopt: disapproval, jeers, and temporary loss of social standing and prestige. (Radin, 1973, 108)

Tribal people valued human life more than nation-states do. For example, to understand the true meaning of the word "warrior," one must understand the balance between individual independence and community responsibility, as discussed earlier in this chapter.

I've read multiple scholarly misinterpretations of warfare in Indian country. But a study of pre-colonial numbers and casualties in inter-tribal warfare provides evidence of far less intense violence compared to Europe. This needs to be historically clarified. Paying attention to cultural differences is critical to eliminating incorrect assumptions and biases.

Two factors limited Indigenous warfare:

1. Native spirituality saw the universe as one; all in the universe were relatives. That did not end conflict between tribes, but it did lessen the number and intensity of inter-tribal conflicts. That is one reason why initial Native contact with Europeans was non-violent. Would the same have been true if circumstances were reversed and Native Americans landed in Europe?
2. Indigenous peoples have a notion of territory, not borders. Borders draw distinct lines, intensifying

nation-state differences and shifting consciousness to the masculine, more aggressive side of our humanity. Tribalism valued feminine/masculine balance in its governance and was less aggressive. Since Native people identified territory but not states with borders, the motive of wars for purposes of expansion did not exist. For example, "mourning wars" simply attempted to replace dead clan members with war captives, a major cause for eastern tribal aggression. On the plains, war was about raiding another people to gain horses or war honors, which included getting close enough to touch the enemy in battle and rescuing a companion in trouble. Killing the enemy would have ranked third as a war honor.

Native Holistic Governance

The Indigenous thought process in council was grounded in the basic physics of the natural world. There was little room for the abstract ideological and political clashes that we see today in Washington and elsewhere.

Years ago, I attended a meeting at the Kansas City Indian Center. A group of parents met to discuss the racism their children were experiencing at school. Their emotions, understandably, were on edge. The various school administrations were not adequately addressing the problem, causing great parental distress and frustration. Before the meeting began, they turned on each other with angry accusations.

A Kiowa Elder at the meeting opened a flat, narrow container and pulled out an eagle feather. The room quieted. Some urban

Indigenous people are unfamiliar with their specific culture these days, but everyone understood what this meant. He then handed the feather to the person on his right. In Indigenous consensus building, each person speaks without interruption or time limit. One may say a word and pass the feather on to the next person, or they may speak for an hour or more. It took well over an hour to go around the circle of the twenty plus parents, with absolutely no interruptions. People actually listened to each other without focusing on their personal response.

When the eagle feather returned to its place of origin, the entire room was, as the Iroquois expression goes, "of one mind"—in complete agreement. When people really listened and understood each other's carefully considered viewpoints, the result was consensus. Even in today's world, this form of Indigenous governance works better than the divisive arguing and politicking of our current political system. The individual ego is tempered by a renewed focus on the well-being of the group.

In Western culture, content is paramount. In tribal North America, there is a balance between content, process, and context. This was illustrated when the Kiowa Elder handed off the eagle feather. The change in process shifted antagonism to acceptance, enabling the circle of arguing parents to reach consensus by listening to all carefully reasoned opinions without interruption.

Indigenous consensus building was grounded by three factors. Aligning thought and action with the physics of the natural world eliminated the dangers of abstract ideological thinking. Coming together with one mind is what happened that night at the Kansas City Indian Center. It also goes a long way to explain why, in 1492, Europe encountered an entire hemisphere that was, unlike

Europe, pristine and thriving with natural life, supporting more than one hundred million human beings, now estimated to be approximately 30% of the world's population at the time.

The central challenge in the meeting was not the racist content of their children's school experience, but rather the issue of communicating in a way that respected the integrity of each individual without interruption. Our culture, even in a city hall meeting I attended, does not provide the same sense of oneness, because the egotistical nature of the committee is always in a hurry to question the speaker and move on. The different atmosphere created in Indigenous council promotes a much more thoughtful and less reactionary approach. Adversarial ire and the need to convince others is diminished. As Martin Luther King Jr. put it, it is better to be "Not a seeker of consensus, but a molder of consensus."

In all my career and volunteer work, I had never experienced unification arising out of dissidence until that night. The lesson is clear: oppositional politics hinders our ability to find common ground and understanding, which are essential for developing solutions. Political agendas and points of view interrupt that process, and that was not what the founding fathers had in mind. A commitment to communicating and working together is critical to the survival of our democracy today.

While disagreement is natural, oppositional politics has intensified over time, leading to the frequent stalemates we now observe in Congress.

Indigenous culture has the ability to build healthy consensus among the people, but it is also a meticulously slow process. It offers individuals freedom of choice, but historically worked to disadvantage Indigenous peoples in the face of the European top-down, rapid decision-making process. Given these culturally diverse factors, it is hard to grasp the level of frustration among tribal people as Euro-Americans took their land. This loss and increasing food scarcity eventually created a survival imperative that caused conflicts among tribes.

Traditional Native Childhood Nurturance

Nurturing children from birth was foundational to the Indigenous governing process.

That nurturing began with a baby's first year of life in a cradle board. Children were swaddled in a soft material like fresh moss, which was changed as needed. This introduced the newborn to the world in a familiar, contained setting while transitioning to living outside the mother's womb. Depending on the specific tribe, babies were taken out of the cradle once a day with slowly increasing frequency.

Cradle boards also served another critical purpose. They were designed to keep the newborn close to their mother and other female relatives as they worked because its design kept them free to move about as the baby remained either propped against a nearby tree or on the mother's back. Under these conditions, babies seldom cried. So began the process of nurturing children into adulthood.

The most critical factor in Indigenous consensus-building democracies was the nurturing of children into adulthood. That process produced the self-confident, mature decision-making described in *Washaka*, the story of Leon Hale's past life, which I discuss below. As an educator, I do not believe the importance of child-rearing can be overemphasized. It was foundational to successful Indigenous organizational structure and is also the key to the health of today's democracy. In the *Exemplar of Liberty: Native America and the Evolution of Democracy*, the link between properly nurtured young adults and a functioning democracy is clearly articulated:

> Robert Rogers, a frontier soldier who studied Indian war tactics and later turned to writing for the press and stage, said that Native children were introduced very early into "public councils," a practice which produced young adults "with a composed and manly air, who were inspired to emulation" and made "bold and enterprising."
>
> Euro-American (and Native American) observers often compared Indian councils to public meetings in Europe and, not uncommonly, found the Indians in better order. (Grinde and Johansen, 2008, 13)

Ben Franklin reflected on this in his comments about Native councils, "To interrupt another, even in Common conversation, is reckon'd highly indecent. How different this is to the conduct of [the] British House of Commons."

Education, parenting, and critical thinking skills were unified. Our survival as a democratic society depends on fostering a similar environment where unification and intelligent decision-making can thrive, achieved through teaching critical thinking and building individuals' self-confidence during childhood.

Raising Children to Self-Actualize

The cultural clash between Indigenous and Western values was profound. It was a clash between a mentality of natural emergence and one of control; a conflict between those who work in partnership with the natural world and those who seek to rise above it.

Native Americans viewed nature as a dynamic force beyond the ability of human comprehension. For example, Native societies believed children were born with a life path bestowed upon them by the forces of creation, and the tribe's responsibility was to create an environment that allowed the child to reach that potential. Foundational to the process of child-rearing was, as expressed in the Anishinaabe (Ojibwa) language, *Gidebweyenimin*, roughly translating to, "I believe in you."

In tribal societies, where the emphasis was on unifying individuals to create a community, children experienced a very different childhood compared to those raised in a nation-state construct. Nation-state societies tend to raise their children through an outside-in process of control that molds the child to the needs of the state. Tribal societies do the opposite. In other words, nation-state parents tend to control their children through adolescence (a developmental stage created during the Industrial Revolution), while traditional tribal societies nurtured their children into adulthood at that age.

Over the past forty years, I have traveled to many Native reservations and met people who have fought against tremendous odds to live with their ancestors in heart and soul. On most reservations in the U.S. and Canada, there are still people who practice their traditional ways despite the pressures to conform to Western norms.

I witnessed firsthand what it means to truly nurture children. By contrast, I was raised with the typical outside-in, controlled approach. The difference in the adults is remarkable.

What does a community that raises its children through nurturance look like? As Margaret Kovach wrote in *Indigenous Methodologies* (52–53), "*Miskâsowin* is a Néhiyaw word that means go to the center of yourself to find your own belonging."

Children Coming of Age

Children in Indigenous communities were nurtured, in contrast to the controlled upbringing common in industrial societies. I call this the tribal "inside-out" as opposed to the Axial "outside-in" approach.

Native children went through a rite of passage into adulthood around the ages of 12 to 14, at which point they were ready for adult responsibilities and marriage. As children were raised through nurturance, they were relatively mature at that age.

The purpose of the rites of passage was to change the status from child to adult, a fully responsible member of the community. Participants were given new names that represented their change in status. Male and female status relationships were separate but equal. After becoming adults through the rites of passage, they attended ceremonies and participated in conferences and councils.

Given this early maturation, the role of tribal Elders in child-rearing cannot be overemphasized. Guidance and wisdom from role models were critical in early child development and maturation.

The Story of Washaka

The book *Washaka: The Bear Dreamer* provides an excellent example of Native childhood nurturance and maturation. When my youngest son worked as a registered nurse on the Cheyenne River Lakota Reservation, he sent me the book.

Author Jamie Lee, while teaching at Oglala Lakota College on the Pine Ridge Reservation, was in a coffee shop "sitting by a window scribbling in a notebook when an Indian man … came to my table and asked if I was a writer." The man introduced himself as Leon Hale. That moment was the beginning of the incredible story of Leon Hale's past life as a young Lakota boy growing up in the mid-19th century on the northern plains.

For years, Hale experienced recurrent dreams about his past life and death. *Washaka* is the compilation of those dreams.

In the story, a young boy named Little Chief (Itancan Cikala) was motivated to solve a problem revealed by a disturbing series of dreams that had plagued him for years. That is why he and his cousin, both 11 years old, slipped out of their village early one morning without the tribe's awareness. This began a journey that challenged both boys to use good judgment in overcoming fear.

When the community discovered the boys were gone, their fathers, uncles, and older cousins secretly tracked them at a distance to ensure their safety. As the journey unfolded, they allowed the boys to make choices and experience the consequences of their actions. Through this type of nurturance, children were allowed to walk their own personal path of maturation while remaining safe.

When they returned home, rather than being punished, the boys' behavior showed the community that they were ready to move forward in their education. The Elders led in analyzing the boys' behavior, determining the best process to move them toward maturation. The two boys learned through personal experience the importance of societal boundaries.

Natural consequences are critical to growth and part of the learning process. Mistakes can be criticized, or they can be used as guidelines for future education. The Lakota Elders turned a potential negative into a positive.

The lessons in the story of *Washaka* are clear. Empower children by allowing them to make reasonable decisions. Let them take risks. At the same time, take safety measures to protect them from injury. Always listen to what the child has to say, and never discount their input and opinions.

An interesting benefit of this nurturing process is that the child grows up with an intellectual depth that is less likely to emerge when the child is continually told what to do and who to be. The self-realization resulting from nurturing is the foundation of self-confidence and sustainability.

This is just scratching the surface of *Washaka*, which I highly recommend. It illustrates why adults raised in that environment could make clear decisions grounded in community responsibility. Hale's story about his past life is an excellent example of how the tribal nurturing process weaves a tapestry of responsible governance and spirituality.

Washaka for the 21st Century

How do we raise children to be adults capable of responsible, intelligent decision-making in today's world? This question reminds me of how my youngest son responded to a nurturing strategy his mother and I used at a key moment in his early life.

We lived in a two-story house with a balcony overlooking the first floor living room. The master bedroom was on one end of the balcony, a sitting room on the other. Because of the distance to his downstairs bedroom, we kept his crib in our room until it was time for him to become more independent. We were concerned it might be "scary" for such a young boy to be all by himself downstairs.

We had already established family meetings with our young son, so he became comfortable expressing himself about issues and solving problems. As the three of us were coming up with a strategy that would give him the courage to move downstairs by himself, suddenly he said, "I have an idea! I could move my bed across the balcony to the sitting room. Then, when I feel comfortable moving downstairs, I'll let you know." We agreed and followed his suggestion. On the third morning, he came to us and said he was ready to move downstairs. From that moment forward, there was never an issue about him sleeping so far away. That was empowerment that resulted from a participatory process. We found that listening to our children's input during inclusive family meetings was essential.

Children who know they are loved can overcome parental errors, so long as they are not too severe. My older son was born when I was only 21 years old and still in college. Fortunately, he survived my lack of maturity into adulthood and is a gifted artist. He and his wife, an attorney, nurture and care for injured and abandoned dogs.

Finding Our Way to Ourselves

This chapter aims to capture the essence of what it means to be Indigenous while attempting to dispel the many stereotypes produced by a people with agendas who did not really know the original peoples of this land. By understanding the humanity inherent in Native American culture, we can reconnect to our own humanity and the depth and sensitivity of which we are all capable of. As Albert Einstein said:

> A human being is part of the whole, called by us Universe … We now experience ourselves, our thoughts and feelings as something separate from the rest … a kind of optical delusion of our consciousness. This delusion is a prison for us. Our task must be to free ourselves from this prison by widening our circle of compassion to embrace all living creatures and the whole of Nature in her beauty.

CHAPTER 5

THE INDIGENOUS WORLDVIEW

Nation-states have proven to be unsustainable. Invariably, once borders are drawn, governance shifts to favor the more aggressive, masculine side of our humanity. This is part of the demise of so-called civilization. Ancient Egypt collapsed or decentralized twice from within, without pressure from outside invading forces. Rome fell from outside forces after years of internal decay. Native America was very different.

Indigenous Community

The concept of Indigenous community is all-encompassing. It is the sense of being one with the energy of the universe and of Mother Earth. This sense is foundational to the Indigenous relationship with the environment, reflected in the concept of sustainability. One should not take more than needed in order to sustain the entire community, and that community encompasses the entire environment, as captured in the Lakota phrase: *Mitakuya Oyasin*. That, at its root, is the meaning of tribalism.

The idea of outward progress and ambition as promoted by

the Euro-American value system is counter to what it means to be Indigenous. Ambition centers on the actions of the individual, while being Indigenous emphasizes the well-being of community. That is why the word "progress," when applied to Native America, relates to the internal development of the individual. This is why Indigenous mythology, as beautifully expressed by N. Scott Momaday, is all about the depth of sensitivity and understanding in each individual within the community.

F. David Peat, quantum physicist at the University of Liverpool, addresses the issue of progress as a Western notion in his book *Blackfoot Physics*. He states, "We have seriously disturbed the balance of nature, sometimes in irreversible ways, and we have a long history of imposing our values on other, less economically powerful societies. Is this an inevitable characteristic of the Western mind?"

Native America viewed a balance of feminine and masculine energy as critical to the tribe's well-being.

Native American Focus on Balance and Harmony Journey to Egalitarianism and Healthy Societies	
Feminine Energy **Inclusivity**	**Masculine Energy** **Exclusivity**
Whole Picture Focus Contextual ○ See the 'Forest' (broad view) ○ Layered Interacting Relationships ○ Social: Community, Agriculture, Council, Home ○ Proper Restraint Ideas and Ideals Group mentality Wisdom and Generosity Symbiotic Relationships	Narrow Focus ○ Separate Entities (Object Orientation) ○ Sees the Trees (specificity) ○ Separates ○ Provider: Hunting, Defending, Crafting, Building, Assisting with Agriculture, Council, etc. Rational and Analytical Practical Action Fortitude and Courage Energy creates growth

Cosmological Understanding

A Native American friend of mine, who served as the physics lecture demonstration director at a major university for forty-one years, once told me that everything he knew about physics he learned from his grandfather while growing up on the Kewa (Santa Domingo) Pueblo. This is because the science of current physics parallels and supports traditional Native spiritual knowledge. They understood the universe operates in a counter force of dualistic energy. Because of this, Native America embraced an ethos of balance and harmony instead of good vs. evil. I imagine my friend's grandfather had a very different approach to physics: one that emphasized being in relationship with nature.

Paintings by the author

A challenge inherent to the human condition is gaining self-awareness that we are active participants in the universe. Native America had an astounding understanding of the universe, and that understanding was the foundation of their spirituality. As F. David Peat wrote:

> Cosmology is not abstracted as a particular branch of Indigenous science but is fully integrated into the unity of nature and all living things, the harmony between the world of spirits and the manifest, the special names and roles of plants and animals and the life-path of each individual. Indigenous cosmology provides a set of values, social integration, and validation for The People.

Peat recognized the Indigenous wisdom that the world is in a constant state of movement, a concept supported by physics. He also identified tribal tricksters (animals) and the sacred clowns in ceremony as beings who reflect that state of flux and the struggle between balance and imbalance.

Native American culture was far more sophisticated than invading Europeans perceived or understood. The tribal worldview embraced inclusivity and promoted sustainability, in stark contrast to a people who had depleted their own land and wanted more.

Staying in Relationship to Time and Motion

The paradox of life is that while we are in constant motion, we are always moving toward physical death. The central challenge of the human condition is to achieve reconciliation, balance, and serenity, allowing death and time to move together in psychological harmony. There is only one certainty in life: nothing will stay the same. One of the spiritual laws of the universe is that nothing is static—motion is constant. Traditional Native American societies acknowledged this cosmic force in their relationships. Their ultimate goal was healthy change that supported both environmental and cultural sustainability.

Spirit World Connection

Traditional Native societies contextualized community issues within the framework of spiritual laws. In Asia, the word "namaste" best captures the meaning of spiritual context. "I honor the light within you. I honor the god within you." The Navajo have a word, *K'a*, which at its root acknowledges the same spiritual understanding.

Historically, if difficult negotiations were to occur in council, traditional Native societies used very specific rituals to lift the burdens from those in council in order to secure a proper context for interaction. For example, the Haudenosaunee/Iroquois ritually removed all of the weariness—the metaphoric thorns, leaves, and other burdens picked up by travelers en route to council—ensuring that communication could proceed calmly. Context is always about the process of interaction. Content is about the subject of that interaction. The Iroquois' preparations for council altered the atmosphere. Egoic self-interest was not a factor, nor was it needed, as everyone knew they would be heard, just as in the meeting at the Kansas City Indian Center mentioned in the previous chapter.

In traditional Native America, the Native council moves in synchronicity with the rhythmic flow of the universe. Often, this is couched in terms of "Indian Time," which acknowledges this creative flux, this state of being in motion—not controlled motion as in clock time, but vibrations of rhythmic time within sacred boundaries of place, that time in motion with the beat of the drum and the rhythmic motion of the dance.

The Red Road

To Native America, all life flows from a single source, a metaphorical hoop. All truths are contained within the sacred hoop, and those truths emanate from the innate intelligence of the universe. The relationship that Indigenous people have with this truth is best expressed in Lakota as *Canku Luta ki*, meaning "the Red Road," or *Canku luta ogana mani*, "I walk the Red Road." The Navajo language has a magnificent way of expressing these understandings with the word *hozho*, which translates to "beauty"—in other words, peace is beauty, health is beauty, blessing is beauty, harmony is beauty, and order is beauty. A series of Navajo ceremonies known as the Beauty Way acknowledge and celebrate these beliefs. This concept was universal among tribes.

Evan T. Pritchard, Mi'kmaq (Micmac) Indian of the Wabanaki Confederacy expressed it this way in his book *No Word for Time, The Way of the Algonquin People*: "The Micmac word *a-glamz* … relates to the Red Road … which … refers to the innate intelligence of the universe. You have to walk the Red Road to find it."

The Red Road challenges humanity to recognize that we are active participants in the universe. We also create, and what we create affects the direction of motion, of energy. That is why the spirit world hears both our prayers and our thoughts.

Quantum physicists have discovered a phenomenon known as the "observer effect," which means that the observation of an object or phenomenon necessarily changes it. Native Americans have known for millennia that humankind is an active participant in the universe. This fosters a profound shared responsibility to maintain balance, which is the foundation of sustainability. Traditional Indigenous rituals acknowledge this shared responsibility.

Euro-American ignorance of Native spirituality is exemplified by a historic incident that occurred during negotiations between Red Cloud of the Oglala Lakota Sioux and the U.S. Government. When Red Cloud requested a temporary pause in the negotiations, he explained that they needed to "go to the buffalo." He was referring to an area in the Black Hills in which the topography formed the shape of a buffalo head.

The government official refused his request even after they were told it meant the Lakota needed to go to the Black Hills to perform their seven Spring Rituals. The Lakota people viewed these rituals as a crucial part of their shared responsibilities in maintaining balance in the universe.

This reveals a fundamental cultural difference. The government official was focused on the meeting's material outcome, while Red Cloud was aligned with the spiritual forces of the natural world.

Spiritual Responsibilities

North American tribal societies engaged in rituals of transformation. These rites of passage included "giveaways" in recognition of accomplishments, ceremonies designed to prepare people emotionally and spiritually to face challenges with courage, and rituals for re-entry into civil society after engaging in war. All

Indigenous ceremonies focus on and foster interpersonal change. Songs, which have great transformative power, are crucial to every step in the process. Native rituals celebrate and honor the transformations that are part of nature's vibrating rhythms. The Red Road is about striving to stay in good relation to the cosmic principles behind everything that is.

Adjusting society to the wisdom discussed in this chapter is not about advanced technology and political dynamics. It is about changes within the individual's relationship to community, the all-encompassing community. Again, changes fall within the guardrails of sustainability, of balance and harmony.

A Holistic View of the Universe

Native America understood that everything in the physical universe is made up of compatible opposites. These are often expressed in terms of feminine and masculine motion or energy. As opposites, a tension forms between them that demands balance and harmony. Balance occurs through a process known as mirroring. Without balance, chaos occurs.

Native American traditions emphasize the responsibility to maintain balance by following the original instructions passed down through each nation's oral tradition. Everything—from organizing the community and raising children to the political system, constructing houses, and conducting rituals—comes from instructions found in each nation's story. These stories reflect the people's cosmological understandings of how the universe is ordered and structured. In her book *Freedom and Culture*, author Dorothy D. Lee wrote that anthropologists sometimes call these "value driven societies" because they are still trying to live by their original instructions.

There is no word for animal in Lakota. The closest word to it is *Wamakaskan*, which translates to all living creatures that move on the earth—two-legged, four-legged, those that crawl, and those that slither. *Wamakaskan* embodies equality in all living beings. Humans are not above animals, because we all came from the same source, and all deserve respect. For example, *Tahca* means deer, *Hehaka* means elk, and *Ikce Wicasha* is human being. All are *Wamakaskan*. We are all equal, all *Wakan*.

What we see in the attempted definitions of the words *Wakan* and *Wamakaskan* is that things are not random. There is no chaos. There is a reason for everything.

Wašíču is the Lakota word for white man. In Lakota spirituality, there is also recognition of that which is unbalanced. The word *Wašíču* is one example. One definition is "takers of the fat," which refers to someone who takes the best parts of a buffalo, denying others the opportunity for those choice portions of meat. In English, it simply means greedy, and that is how they saw the white man: those who do not share.

This explains why most Native American societies were/are structured to foster political and social equality for both women and men. The human community mirrors the universe when feminine and masculine qualities are in balance.

Due to the linguistic differences between European and Indigenous languages, making exact translations is challenging because their multiple layers of meaning shift depending on context. For example, a mystery is expressed by the word *Wakan*, which means the beginning of everything that is. Native spirituality goes all the way back to that original "mystery." There is no word in the English language that can properly define *Wakan*. The Jesuits translated it as "sacred." They were not wrong, but that missed the point. *Wakan* is more layered and specific in meaning. It is the birth of dualistic energy and motion. *Kan* comes from the word *skan*, which means motion. Perhaps the closest we can come to the meaning is the term "the big bang theory." *Wakan* reflects a deep understanding of the universe's beginning.

Everything is *Wakan*, in constant motion—from the atoms in your chair, to the energy in the sun, to your heartbeat and the heartbeat of Mother Earth, to the stars, the rivers, and the spirit world. At the very center, at the source of all motion, creation is complete, in total stillness—a mirror of opposites and compatibility.

Indigenous spirituality was anchored in the laws of physics and accepted the limitations of the human mind. For example, *Wakan* ranged from the ancient (back to the very beginning of time) to things beyond human comprehension, the spiritual, and the unknown. It is the ultimate, undefined source of all that exists.

And you can experience it without understanding or explaining it.

Wakan is why Indigenous cultures do not attempt to define a god or portray a creator beyond human comprehension. It is a recognition of the limits of the human mind to define the ultimate source of everything that is. It is foundational to the Indigenous sense of intellectual and spiritual humility and is grounded in reality—neither science nor organized religion has uncovered the reason for the creation of the universe.

No explanation of *Wakan* is ever complete, because in Native spirituality, each individual's understanding is unique, growing over their entire lifetime. This discussion represents my understanding after 40 years of participation, but I cannot speak for others.

The Indigenous holistic worldview is deeply embedded in their language. As discussed previously, Native languages are syllabic. Each syllable expresses a complete idea, and together they form another concept, with the dualistic thought process generating meaning on both levels. Thus, the word for grandfather also signifies the beginning of the universe, all the way back to *Wakan.* It is a mistake to project Euro-American thought processes into Indigenous cultures: they are just too different!

When I think of visiting the Sistine Chapel and looking up at Michelangelo's ceiling painting of God reaching out to Adam, I am reminded of the extreme diversity of the human intellect. The painting illustrates a linear-binary thought process compared to the more holistic Indigenous view that accepts and embraces infinity without trying to define or picture it.

Indigenous Definition of Wealth

Materialistic societies define wealth in terms of material possessions. The Indigenous peoples in this hemisphere had an entirely different view. Wealth and status were measured in terms of what could be given to community.

This was woven into song, dance, drums—the "heartbeat of Mother Earth"—and ceremony. Wealth was felt within oneself, rooted in one's relationship to community and the natural world. Individuals' strengths came together to create a community that was close-knit and connected, and where there was weakness, others filled the void. By definition, that is community.

Giveaways: The Soul of Holistic Living in Native North America

Those cultural differences on how wealth is perceived can lead to a misunderstanding of giveaways, an Indigenous cultural phenomena found in every Native American nation throughout North America. To the Western eye, giveaways redistribute wealth to minimize tribal social stratification. Native peoples understood the benefit of redistribution, but viewed it in a spiritual context, as a manifestation of the sense of oneness with all that exists.

I once visited the Santa Clara Pueblo during one of their "feast days" with Kachina dances. As a stranger, I found myself welcomed into homes and offered food. Every household invited me to join them. In this process of Feeding the People, metaphor and metaphysics merge and go right to the soul of community as a way of sharing wealth with others. Food sustains the body, and thus, Feeding the People speaks to the core of what it means to be a community. It was a loving, friendly experience and gave me a deep sense of community.

Giveaways occur at Native American celebrations and spiritual events, including powwows, vision quests, and name-giving ceremonies, to list just a few examples. To Native peoples, all these events convey meanings that reach far beyond the material concerns of the Western culture. The giveaway is a way of mirroring Mother Earth, and how she provides for our wants and needs unconditionally. She only asks for acknowledgement of her gifts and a thank you, just as you would expect from your own children. Wisdom and knowledge of the great spiritual laws of the universe offer one constraint: support sustainability by not taking anything that cannot regenerate itself. This is the spiritual and philosophical base for Native subsistence economies. The giveaway is an expression of the teachings of Mother Earth and an example of the spiritual guidance gained through the process of mirroring.

Gift giveaways engage the sponsoring family in a spiritual process of preparation and gratitude. The gifts are not viewed as objects but as metaphors for the meaning behind the relationships.

It can take a family a year or more to assemble the items and prepare them to move through the community. Historically, items were handmade with the wants and needs of specific individuals in mind. Thus, gifts were personal and represented deeply caring relationships. The gifts could move to others at future giveaways, as an acknowledgement of those relationships. This re-gifting was a form of relationship awareness and growth. Today, items are both handmade and bought, with blankets being one of the most purchased items.

There is yet another dimension to this practice. Giveaways honor someone's accomplishments, acknowledge a new name, or serve as a memorial to honor someone who has passed on. As gifts move, they become symbols of either joy or remembrance, and as such, they bind the community together. Their movement through the community creates powerful unseen threads of commitment and loving care.

Giveaways can also take the form of informal gift giving during a Feed the People meal after Inipi ceremonies, or they may take on more formality. Often at powwows, someone introduces the sponsoring family and explains the purpose of the giveaway. This is a time of honoring through oratory, bringing the community together in a shared purpose. Then a song is sung honoring the sponsoring family as they begin to dance in a sunwise direction around the circle. The circle was a key Native concept because it is holistic—without beginning or end. Everything is connected in a state of complete unification. The circle is the sacred hoop of life and appeared in everything, from the rotation of the earth around the sun to the sun itself. Even the buffalo that Native people of the plains followed traveled in a circle.

Supporters enter the circle, shake hands with the family, offer a gift of their own, and then dance behind the family. As an Apache once explained, "Music is the blood of our culture. Without music, we would not have an *Indé* (Apache) soul."

When the circle is complete and the song is finished, the sponsoring family gathers by the speaker's stand to distribute gifts to individual community members. As gifts move through the community, bonds are strengthened.

The idea of wealth is not found in the gifts, but in the dancing and celebration of family and community woven into the rich tapestry of cultural identity.

These practices illustrate the differences between the Native ethos from the Western perspective. It is a common and very misleading mistake to project Western motivations into Indigenous cultures.

The Circle of Indigenous Life

There is consistency in the Indigenous worldview, from the Lakota word *hocaka* for space captured within the circle, to the

Mi'kmaq *a-glamz*, the Red Road, and the Natural Way, to the eagle feather passed around the circle at the Kansas City Indian Center. That consistency reflects the holistic view of Indigenous life from coast-to-coast in North America and its relationship to the energy of the universe. It is the circle of life. To the Indigenous peoples, that is the real world.

CHAPTER 6

METAPHOR: THE MIND THAT SEES IN RELATIONSHIP

We are a spirit, we are a natural part of the earth, and all of our ancestors, all of our relations who have gone to the spirit world, they are here with us.
That's power.
They will help us.
They will help us see if we are willing to look.

—John Trudell, Santee Dakota

Metaphor is a story form used by the ancients, and its depth and sophistication challenge the notion that "time equals progress." The idea that modern humanity is advanced is flawed; we are only advanced if we define it through the lens of materialism and technology.

But there is so much more to our humanity.

Oral tradition over thousands of years kept the history of the people alive. Prayer, ritual, dance, art, and music were all part of a living culture reflected in metaphor.

Story Metaphor

Kiowa author N. Scott Momaday, cited in Chapter 5, provides an example of the deeper, whole brain thinking nurtured through metaphor in his story *The Arrowmaker*. Passed down through generations, the storyline appears simple, focusing on a Kiowa couple in their tipi. The man, an arrowmaker, suddenly senses someone outside. He speaks in an even tone, as if to his wife, but is actually speaking to the unknown stranger, "*If you are a Kiowa, you will understand what I am saying, and you will speak your name.*" This is both a question and a request for confirmation because their safety is at stake. When the outsider doesn't respond, it confirms the arrowmaker's suspicion that the stranger is not Kiowa, and he shoots him through a slight opening in the tipi cover. In that moment, after those brief words, order and well-being are restored.

Momaday explains that the story, told many times by his father, took on new meanings through the passing years and adds, "*I am sure that I do not yet understand it in all of its consequent meanings.*" Such is the power of metaphor.

He goes on to say that Native stories are part of an oral tradition that continues intergenerationally as long as there is someone to speak and someone to listen. "That is to say, it has been neither more nor less durable than the human voice, and neither more nor less concerned to express the meaning of the human condition." He believes everything rests on the understanding of language, adding, the "story of *The Arrowmaker* is supremely metaphorical."

Momaday and the story of *The Arrowmaker* reveals the importance of metaphor in understanding Indigenous culture. To derive meaning from the metaphors in Native stories requires a sense of wholeness in heart, mind, and spirit, revealing the depth of the Indigenous spirit.

Metaphor: Connection to Place

Traditional Native peoples are in relationship with their homelands. Where I now live was once the homeland of the Niutachi people. Niutachi roughly translates to "people where two rivers merge," referring to where the Kansas River flows into the Missouri. When people are in harmony with the natural world around them, metaphors emerge and become integrated into the culture. This is why it is difficult for people in industrialized nation-states to understand metaphor, as they do not have that close relationship with their homeland.

Why is metaphor so connected to a people's sense of oneness with place? On the surface, metaphors may seem to only be fantasy, but as one matures, they draw the listener into the spiritual reality of intricate human relationships with nature. It involves and encourages a whole brain process and depth of thought, as it expresses in abstract terms those interacting relationships and our oneness with the universe.

Metaphor nurtures the human mind into maturity. Paradoxically, metaphors eventually open the mind to experiencing the facts of reality, rather than a myriad of opinions expressed as fact, as they connect the spiritual nature of our humanity to our behavior and our relationship to place—specifically, to one's homeland. Gregory Cajete in his book *Native Science: Natural Laws of Independence*, explains that Elders in Pueblo societies frequently use metaphors to communicate, and that those metaphors emerge out of the context of place.

Metaphor in Music

Traditional Indigenous music is spiritual, embodying the metaphoric rhythm and unified motion of the universe. The drum is the heartbeat of Mother Earth. The masculine side of our humanity integrates the rhythm of that heartbeat into the energy emanating from Mother Earth. In the music played by the Plains tribes, women stand behind the men at the drums, adding their voices to create balanced feminine/masculine unification.

Native dance is also a metaphor of unity. The dancers in regalia move with the universe's rhythmic time. Masculine and feminine energies merge as the dancers move with that heartbeat.

In contrast, most Euro-American music has evolved from a spiritual consciousness to an entertainment medium.

Metaphor in the Visual Arts

As our Western minds try to understand Indigenous design, we ask ourselves: Is it "art?" Is it decoration? It seems attractive, but what does it mean? Euro-American art has a purpose: to express beauty or reflect an ideal, as seen in movements like Abstract Expressionism.

How is Indigenous design a different kind of expression?

There is a clear difference between an object-oriented mentality and that which is grounded in spirituality and relationships.

It is important here to make a distinction between items made by hand and those mass produced.

Today, many Native artists continue the ancient traditions, prioritizing spiritual relationship over profit. Their work reflects clear understanding that metaphor, spirituality, process, and design are inseparable. And as discussed in the Linguistics chapter, those concepts are also woven into the fabric of Indigenous languages. Even process itself is metaphor that connects Indigenous spirituality, thought, and motion.

One may wonder why I selected story and music to bridge into Indigenous "art." The answer is that "art" is not Indigenous. In fact, Native languages had no word for art. What we think of as Native art is actually a visual language loaded with symbols and design metaphors.

In fact, the modern concept of art did not exist in any culture until 16th century Europe during the Renaissance and the Newtonian era. Even so, in my hometown, the Nelson-Atkins Museum of Art in Kansas City, Missouri, has six Native American "art" galleries.

So, what qualities or criteria define a piece as a work of art? Five categories are often used in definition: line, shape, color, texture, and space. All relate to appearance. In applying these criteria, it is easy to understand why modern art scholars often define what Indigenous people have historically produced as art.

But in the Indigenous mind, those pieces were a visual metaphor that expressed their beliefs and view of the universe as an interconnected family. Native culture was full of aesthetically pleasing designs, and those designs had deep metaphorical meanings. Art historian David W. Penney described it this way: "When reading about the myriad of ways in which the visual arts were involved in the very fabric of Native American society, one may perhaps begin to sense that the word 'art' is an inadequate term to describe the remarkable objects created by a unique group of people."

It is challenging for the Western mind to develop a full appreciation of traditional Native American design. Not only are shapes full of meaning, but color combinations and spacing can change the metaphorical meaning of designs just as Indigenous languages unified single syllabic concepts into a new dynamic.

For example, you can usually identify tribal provenance through design and color relationships in pieces produced during the 19th century. If one can identify which tribe created a given design and color combination, one may be able to understand the metaphorical meanings of such design.

However, designs may have as many as three layers of metaphorical meaning, of which we can only interpret the most obvious. Along with the more general interpretations, sometimes a given community has meanings specific to them. On yet another level, a lineage within the community may be associated with a specific design and color combination.

The visuals of Native design are as conceptually sophisticated as Momaday's story of *The Arrowmaker* with its complex layers of metaphor. Those of us who were not raised in an ancient Indigenous culture must be satisfied with the more surface-level interpretation of each design, knowing that those designs likely have even more meanings specific to different tribal lineages or clans.

In the Kansas City region, the ancient homeland of the

Niukonska Wazhazhe (Osage) or "people of the Middle Waters," was mostly south of the Missouri River. Garrick Bailey and Daniel C. Swan's book *Art of the Osage* includes excellent research on Indigenous design interpretation that can, in concept, be applied to most North American Indigenous peoples. They explain: "Osage arts are based on a highly organized philosophy and a worldview that embraces a keen sense of duality expressed through sets of paired oppositions.... Bisected forms often occur in contrasting light and dark colors, such as red and blue, which are symbolic of the duality of the cosmos."

For example, the Nelson-Atkins Museum has a beaded Seminole bag that expresses dualistic energy in the different designs on each strap. The bag itself holds meaning as well. To the woman who crafted the bag around 1830, it represented the reconciliation of the universe's dualistic energy forces—between the heavens and earth, feminine and masculine. The energy of those relationships reconciles in the pouch design, which merges the energy of both sources. This reflects the philosophical basis for the Indigenous values of balance and harmony, rooted in the reconciliation of the duality present in the universe.

Major design concepts include duality and reconciliation; transformation; relationship (clan identity and community); the spirituality of daily living, tied to natural laws, seasonal cycles, and rhythmic time; and sacred numbers.

What is "Sophisticated"?

Ancient Mississippian pots may look simple to the untrained eye. But the functional simplicity of design and expertise in firing reflects a highly sophisticated understanding of the relationship between earth and sun. Many pottery designs appear to be intentional and reflect the potter's understanding of the interacting relationships within nature. The firing process used positioning and the forest breezes to create designs on the pots. The result is both beautiful and graceful and embodies the oneness of sun, air, earth, and the human mind.

Shards from older pots were often added to temper the clay and connect to the ancestors. It reflected a mind that thinks, "I am because we are."

Visual Duality

Years ago, my youngest son and I created this illustration to explain to a college class I was teaching about the Indigenous concept of how the universe established order out of dualistic forces. White and black, as opposing colors, represent opposing energies. In merging the two, gray is produced. Neither extreme can make its way through both colors, but the mixed color of gray survives both extremes. The gray reveals a reconciliation of those extremes, just as the reconciled dualistic energy of the universe creates order and balance, as we saw in the Seminole bag description above.

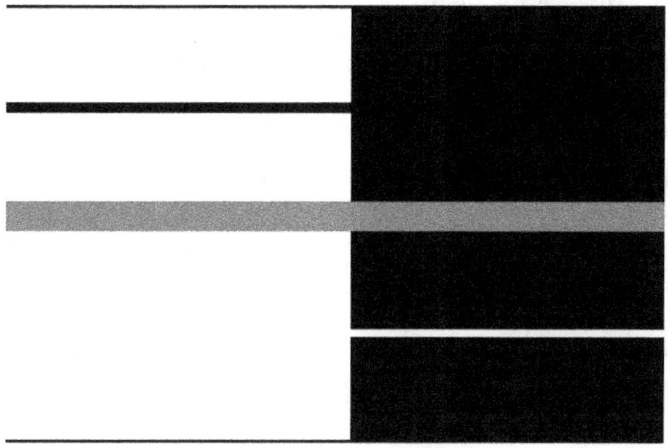

In the same manner, atoms are made up of positive and negative electrical charges. The protons in the nucleus are positive charges, and the electrons revolving around the nucleus are negative charges. The electrons are held in place by the reconciliation of two forces: weak force pushing out of the nucleus against a strong force pushing toward the nucleus. We see this often in Native designs.

As Garrick Bailey and Daniel C. Swan wrote in their book *Art of the Osage*: "The orderly presentation of oppositional forms paired in overall designs is further enriched by the paradox that often results from the unpredictability of natural forces—things are not always what they first appear to be" (196).

They go on to say that a closer look reveals no foreground or background. The two designs are no longer oppositional. Together they tell the story of the universe.

Dualistic energy is often referred to in feminine/masculine terms. Color designates which energy form is represented.

Consistent Cross-Tribal Values

A second artifact in the Nelson-Atkins Museum is an Osage blanket. It was made 1,000 miles northwest of where the Seminole bag was created, and one hundred years later. And yet, accounting for cultural differences in design, space, and time, the two reflect the same understanding of the universe.

The colors in both objects are metaphors. The base color of the blanket is blue, which expresses calm. There are four images of light blue hands outlined in white. The hands represent the family, while the white outlines symbolize peace and protection. A zig-zag pattern framing the blue signifies lightning—the coming storm. But in the blue rectangle, the family is safe. The lightning also reminds us that accompanying rain nurtures life, providing sustainability through unified action. Two borders of yellow, green, and red signify birth, life, and eternity.

Once again, the design reflects the basic Indigenous values of balance and harmony—the values of sustainability.

And so, in Indigenous design, we see the reconciliation of nature's dualistic forces. That energy occasionally explodes due to imbalance, exemplified by events like a tsunami, hurricane, or volcanic eruption. And then, that destructive energy is reconciled, with this reconciliation serving as the foundation of Indigenous intellectual sophistication. That intellectual depth is embodied in Indigenous design and the inherent beauty of Native oral tradition, as reflected in Momaday's book *The Man Made of Words*. Momaday's work as a writer and poet dances in partnership with Indigenous visual design—in rhythm to the beat of metaphor—with all its depth of meaning that embodies the traditional Indigenous cultures.

History is not just events divided into tidy categories; it is an interwoven tapestry of cultural complexity. In this tapestry's dualistic design, we see the beauty of our humanity in balance with the dualistic forces of the universe. The rhythmic motion melds with Momaday's oration and the wisdom of Indigenous ancestors, encapsulating what it means to be Indigenous and connected in that sense of relationship with time and place.

Understanding Spiritual Context

Discussing a spiritual experience out of context (for example, in this book), is inappropriate because it diminishes the spirituality of the experience. Indigenous spirituality offers a depth of knowing that can only be gained through direct experience—it is beyond the ability of the written word to capture.

Indigenous spirituality is experiential, not academic, and it is sophisticated, not simple. It is not for everyday conversation, and it represents a cultural experience that is easy to misinterpret. In Native societies, it is only appropriate to discuss certain spiritual experiences when medicine people, who have a deep understanding of Indigenous spirituality, are present. Without their presence, it would be like trying to explain quantum field theory to a novice in five minutes by phone. The theory would have no meaning without the experience.

The cultural gap between Indigenous peoples and those of Euro-America is vast. Traditional Native spirituality views the universe's energy in motion through reconciliation of duality into a singularity. In contrast, Western thought sees a universe of exclusivity—a universe focused on comparative difference, not singularity. A profound example of that difference is found in two descriptions of an ancient Mimbres pot in the book *To Touch the Past: The Painted Pottery of the Mimbres People*. The individual analysis by the authors (non-Native scholar of Mimbres ceramic arts, J. J. Brody, and Tewa Indigenous scholar Rina Swentzell) are stunningly different. Swentzell's description included the bowl's spiritual connection to the woman it was buried with, whose head pointed east.

The difference in perception and explanation is stunning, with the intellectual focus worlds apart: one reflects objectification for analytical purposes, while the other attempts to understand the spiritual significance.

Brody	Swentzell
"This dynamic overall pattern is structured simultaneously as a two-part and four-part composition. In the two-part structure, each half opposes the other in a bifold, symmetrical arrangement; as a four-part one, an A-B-A-B pattern revolves radially around a center point."	"In modern Pueblo thought, swirls indicate the breath, or life, which moves much as smoke does—not in a straight line but in curls and twists. This design hints at the cosmic breath flowing from the pyramidal mountain forms into the valley, which contains sun and moon as a circular background."

Sacred Clowns

In many tribes, sacred clowns, who represent the dualistic nature of the universe, guarded Native communities from overly ambitious leaders. Today, they provide teachings about chaos and order as they create disruption and imbalance while participants in a ceremony ignore them to maintain balance. If a leader becomes too arrogant, he will undoubtedly find a sacred clown walking behind him, mimicking and exaggerating his acts as observers laugh at the clown's antics. It would be highly embarrassing for any leader to be followed by a clown.

The stripes on the *Koshare* (Pueblo clowns) represent the reconciliation of duality in the universe. When I was at San Ildefonso Pueblo, the clowns at a Corn Dance served two roles. They maintained order among the dancers, but when the dancing stopped, their behavior changed to act out the disruption and imbalance of mankind.

Related to the tradition of the sacred clown is the "trickster," a mystical character such as Raven in the Northwest Coastal regions and *Iktomi* (spider) in the Lakota region. They provide examples of chaos and order, of proper status-relationship conduct. By acting out the dualism of chaos and order, they establish spiritual boundaries on community behavior. They represent an indirect approach to maintaining order while also establishing a proper relationship between the clans and tribal leadership.

Architectural Dualism Reflected Astrological Understanding

The turnoff from the main highway to get to Chaco Canyon is located about twenty miles from Farmington, New Mexico, followed by another twenty miles of dirt and gravel roads. The canyon contains seventeen buildings and ancient roads leading from the canyon to a number of outlier towns, some located as far as 60 miles away, all constructed between 700 and 1200. Each building physically aligns to a solar or lunar cycle. One building in the canyon, Pueblo Bonito, was five stories high.

In front of the canyon's mouth, about a mile away, is Fajada Butte. An ancient spiral chiseled on the butte's vertical wall represents the most unique measurement of time in the world, in this case, time in infinity, bisected by a dagger of sunlight. That light happens once a year when the sun reaches the summer solstice. Then it moves south to the equinox. The day the sun reaches the equator, two light daggers frame the entire spiral, precisely measuring the seasonal movement of the sun.

The spiral also measures the lunar cycle, which takes a little over 18 years to complete. Once a year, light from the moon aligns with a line in the circle. Each year it moves out one line toward the last (ninth) line. Then it begins to reverse one line at a time back to the center. On the 18th year, it reaches the center of the circle. To date, there is no known measure of both solar and lunar cycles on one spiral anywhere else in the world. That one spiral on Fajada Butte relates to the construction of every building in Chaco Canyon as well as to all the outlier towns. Here we see entire buildings as metaphor to the motions of earth, moon, and sun.

Transformation and Spirituality

The *Diné* (Navajo) ceremonial basket is often called a "wedding basket," but its function is much broader. It tells the Navajo creation story, rich with layers and spiritual nuances, and the design represents a map of our life journey. In the very center of the basket is the *sipapu*, through which the *Diné* people, like many of their pueblo neighbors, emerged from a prior world into this world. The white in the center represents birth. As you travel around the coils (reminiscent of the Fajada Butte spiral) moving outward, you begin to encounter black. The black represents darkness, challenge, struggle, and pain. As you make your way around the coils, you eventually reach the red bands, which represent marriage, the mixing of blood through family unity. The red is pure—during this time there is no darkness. But, moving forward, life transitions back into darkness interspersed with white light—moments of enlightenment amongst dark bands—until finally you reach all white. I can imagine tribal Elders collected in the white coils at the edge of the basket. The outer coil is there as a reminder that no matter how much darkness you encounter in life, there is always a pathway to the light. The layers of interpretation continue: "The outward spiral of the design emulates our journey into wisdom. It holds within its structure the balance of the feminine and masculine energy—both energies in proper alignment with which we create new life" (Natural History Museum of Utah).

Masks: A Flow of Energy

The early seeds for the social science of ethnohistory were planted by anthropologists like William N. Fenton in the 1930s. Fenton grew up in western New York, close to the Allegheny Seneca reservation. He conducted a detailed study on Iroquois face society (masking). He tried to categorize the masks but found a fluidity in the Native practices that prevented him from categorizing them. Masks were used for multiple purposes and ceremonies, challenging the Euro-American linear-binary thought process of categorization.

Masks Tell Stories

One of the cedar masks in my collection was carved by Tony Hunt Jr., a member of the internationally recognized Hunt family who are Kwakiutl artists of the Northwest coast. The mask reflects an ancient legend about two men sitting by a fire. One bragged about his affluence as he tossed a valuable item into the fire to display his wealth. The other, aiming to prove his superiority, tossed something even finer into the fire. This back and forth continued until one of the men picked up a valuable copper shield and threw it into the fire. When he did so, the flames exploded, burning half of his face and marking it with traces of copper. The message is clear. Excess is dangerous; duality must remain in balance. The masterfully done carving reflects both the concepts of duality and the destructiveness of imbalance.

The Wisdom of a Zuni Kiva Bowl

A friend of mine has a Kiva ceremonial bowl which represents the dynamics of spiritual transformation into oneness.

The bowl functions at the whole brain level of thought necessary for complex metaphor, rather than the linear thinking required to construct a materially complicated object like a jet airplane. The Euro-American linear thought process sees the jet as a symbol of progress. But when looking at the wisdom depicted on the bowl, we see intellectual depth of thought and sophisticated understanding that reaches far beyond the object itself. Native thought processes try to be "part of" the world while the Euro-American process tries to "rise above" it with new objects/technology. This illustrates a fundamental difference in these two human value systems.

What story does the bowl tell? There are four stair-step formations around the rim that represent the directional spiritual forces. Tadpoles on the inside and outside of the bowl are heading toward two water serpents, which the Zuni call *Kolowissi.* The serpents are a metaphor for water and transformation. A frog appears on the other side of the water serpents in the bowl's center. The tadpole passing through the water serpent has transformed into a frog. The spirit of the frog represents an understanding of the dynamics of the river and the land. The bowl conveys that through spirituality and ritual, we transform into balance and harmony, fostering sustainability for the community and its continuity in partnership with the dynamics of change.

Multiple Meanings in a Tularosa Pot ca. 1200–1400

One of my pots was found in the ancient ruins of a house just west of the Zuni Pueblo in Arizona. Around the opening of the pot is a design that non-Natives often interpret as arrows, but this is a Euro-American cultural projection. The design actually depicts bird tracks. These allude to an ancient Puebloan legend about thirsty people roaming the desert, desperately looking for water, when a Swift flew above them and said, "Follow me. I will take you to water." The bird tracks circle the opening of the water container and then walk or move into the swirls of eternal time, reflecting the interconnection and sense of oneness we saw in the Fajada Butte spiral. Although there are many layers of interpretation in this complex design, any attempt to define what the woman potter was thinking eight hundred years ago would be theoretical at best.

Inside the pot, the woman created ridges with her fingers to make the inner surface larger than the outer surface. This was done to stabilize the internal water temperature in the desert heat. Despite this, our current society would call her and the pot primitive.

Nature and Ceremonial Metaphor

The Hamat'sa dance on the Northwest Coast of Canada is a ceremony that initiates boys into adulthood. After spending a year or so out in the forest surviving on their own, they reenter society as adults through a ceremony that reintroduces them as civil tribal members. The ceremony is vital for transforming the young men from a state of imbalance to balance, and from isolation to becoming healthy, active members of Kwakwaka'wakw (Kwagulth) society.

On one of my visits to the west coast of Vancouver Island, I had the privilege of meeting a man who had gone through the "rite of passage" sojourn in the forest and reentered Kwakwaka'wakw society. He was alone in the forest for nine months, completely self-reliant for food, shelter, and clothing. He remembered learning something about himself each time he faced a challenge, working through his emotions and pushing ahead. When he returned to society, the Hamat'sa ceremony prepared him to reenter the community as a man of civility.

This man and others took me out into the ocean in a traditional twenty-foot canoe. It was remarkable how peaceful the canoe ride felt, accompanied by only the sound of water, sea gulls, and an eagle, with the waves embracing the sides of the canoe as we seemed to slide through ocean. By the time we returned to shore, I felt completely at peace. Connected to the ocean that day, I gained insight into Indigenous psychological health and stability.

I also learned about the incredible knowledge needed to navigate a "living" ocean in a large canoe. I learned what rhythmic time was and how critical it is to understanding nature. There are jokes about "Indian time," but when it comes to traversing the ocean, Indian time is incredibly precise. In the ocean, there are channels that flow at different speeds and directions, which one must learn how to navigate. The channels change depending on the time of day and season due to Earth's relationship to the moon's gravitational pull—another reminder that we are all one with the universe. These experiences are invaluable to my understanding of Indigenous spirituality.

Intellectual Depth in Metaphoric Design

I met Haida artist Lionel Samuels in Victoria B.C. Most of the Haidas live on Haida Gwaii (Queen Charlotte Islands), about eighty miles off the coast of the British Columbia mainland. I obtained a limited-edition print from him that captures an important Northwest Coast Haida myth. It tells the story of a powerful chief who sustained a world of darkness because he kept the sun, moon, and the stars in a secret cedar box. The description that accompanied the picture reads:

> Raven decided to trick the chief out of these treasures by turning himself into a spruce needle which was swallowed by the chief's sister while she was drinking water at a creek. The girl became pregnant and before long gave birth to Raven in human form. The boy, who was the pride and joy of the chief, eventually coaxed the chief into letting him play with the treasures in the box. When the time was right, the boy Raven turned back into his bird form and flew thru the smoke hole of the chief's house with the sun, the moon and the stars. Now all the world could share in the great gift of light.

The picture conveys powerful metaphors about the trickster spirit Raven and the duality of feminine and masculine energy in relation to water. This is exemplified by a story recounting how the chief's sister drank creek water and swallowed a spruce needle, representing transformation.

Using metaphor to take the viewer back to the origins of all that is, Lionel Samuels depicts the directional spiritual powers emerging from the box, releasing light into the darkness.

Does it relate to the "big bang" theory in modern physics? Though it is hard to speculate on the knowledge of the ancients, much that is expressed in Native metaphoric design seems to parallel current scientific knowledge. The Native process of gaining knowledge differs greatly from the scientific method, leading us to ask the question: how did they know?

Reviving the Power of Tradition

I purchased a salmon club from traditional Cowichan sculptor Simon Charlie on the reserve next to Duncan, British Columbia, Vancouver Island. The club was designed to kill salmon and depicts a seal feeding on a salmon. The spirit of the seal is carved as a face on the belly of the seal.

Like so many Indigenous cultures, the Cowichan people suffered deeply from colonization, enduring tragedies such as boarding schools (called residential schools in Canada) and being forced to abandon their traditional cultures. It is remarkable that in so many tribes, one individual refused to comply with the pressure and continued the ancient traditions. Sculptor Simon Charlie was that person for the Cowichan people on Vancouver Island.

As years went by, young Cowichan men became interested in learning their ancestral traditions and began to gather around Simon Charlie's little house and studio. Today, many Cowichan carvers work in the ancient traditions thanks to this one individual who refused to succumb to the pressures exerted by Euro-American society. There is now a very impressive Cowichan Cultural Center in Duncan, with totem poles carved by students of Simon Charlie around the city. Two poles frame the entrance of Duncan's City Hall: one from the Māori people of New Zealand and the other is from the Cowichan. Together, they represent an Indigenous connection across the Pacific Ocean. Simon Charlie embodied the strength to maintain one's identity even in the face of extreme pressure—the strength of being Indigenous.

A Tradition of Giving

I bought a pot from my friend Phil Shifflet. At one time, Phil lived in San Ysidro, New Mexico, a small village between the Zia and Walatowa (Jemez) Pueblos. He was a builder by profession. One day, during a visit with Seferina Bell, the matriarch potter of the Zia Pueblo, Phil quietly noticed electrical issues in her home. The next morning, he appeared at her door carrying all the tools he needed to repair the problems. By afternoon, the work was complete. He did not charge her for this work. As he prepared to leave, Seferina unexpectedly gave him one of her large handmade, painted, and fired pots. This story reflects what it truly means to be Indigenous. Neither anticipated the other's actions, which held deeper meanings beyond the actions themselves.

A few years before I met Phil, I had visited Seferina. As I looked at her pots, to my surprise, she suggested another Zia potter who also made fine pottery. In that moment, I felt what it means to be Indigenous in community—a sense of oneness with all that is. She was not in egotistical competition with her neighbor.

Over the years, since being adopted into my Dakota family in South Dakota and participating in Indigenous ceremonies, I have come to realize what it truly means to be Indigenous, to be part of a community, to be tribal. My journey through Indigenous America began forty years ago, and I have never forgotten their gift of initiation.

Seferina and Phil have passed on now, but the priceless

understandings they gifted me have not. And that flow continues in this writing and, perhaps, into infinity.

As I sit in front of the laptop in the library of my home, I glance out the window at the forest that I share with a community college. It is fall, and the forest is full of yellow leaves. It is absolutely beautiful. As Nimkii Kwe-Anishinaabe said, "Trees are the IT girls of our ecosystem. They sequester carbon and give us clean breath."

It is this sense of oneness that connects these beautiful works of Native culture—Indigenous philosophy grounded in the laws of physics that transformed into works of art. Fall flows into winter, winter into spring, and then back to summer, just as the spiral on the Chaco Canyon Butte and Indigenous pottery continue to reflect eternal, cyclical time. When my mind drifts to that beauty, I see a world of peace, one that is interconnected with everything in the universe.

CHAPTER 7

THE CULTURAL ETHOS OF STORYTELLING

I would so immerse myself in that era and that person's thought and read their language until I would see through their eyes. That's why I emphasize how important it is to have a kind of sympathetic imagination to enter into world views of other times and other people.

—Richard Tarnas, Ph.D., "A Brief History of Western Thought Part 2 of 5"

Years ago, I heard a Stanford professor give a talk on Cheyenne star knowledge. He showed a historic buffalo robe painted with star patterns that represented the heavens. The stars were placed accurately for that time and location. I listened, mesmerized for ninety minutes, as he detailed the Cheyenne star knowledge depicted on this robe, which reflected our relationship to the heavens. That lecture helped me understand that Native mythologies manifest out of natural phenomena. From the stars to the storyteller, the audience learned what it meant to be one with all that is.

The Native cultural process thrived on a rich oral tradition, and after years of contemplation, I still wonder: is literacy truly superior, or just a reflection of cultural bias? A personal relationship with the storyteller adds content to the story in the form of voice inflection and body language that is absent in the written word if without detailed description.

Metaphor in Story

Metaphor is powerful because it reveals patterns rather than getting lost in detail. The challenge for modern-day listeners is to understand metaphor: to see the images in Indigenous narrative as symbols of deeper meanings, and to see what they represent, just as the star map reflected a depth of understanding I had never imagined before. This was also true of their stories.

As discussed in the previous chapter, metaphor represents or is symbolic of something else, especially something abstract. And that was true of stories across Native America.

Indigenous creation stories were shared over thousands of years. Listeners of all ages, surrounded by the sounds of the natural world, "saw" in their mind's eye a reality that grew from the concrete to the metaphysical and spiritual. The stories reflected metaphorical relationships to the universe.

One reason metaphor was common in ancient stories is that there was a greater sense of community. All age levels sat around the storyteller, and metaphors spoke to everyone. In addition, metaphors also take the human mind beyond "knowledge" to a deeper sense of "knowing."

Education at Multiple Depths

Context was critical to many stories in the Indigenous oral traditions. Native stories were often told in relation to a specific time or place. Some were told only in the wintertime during the winter solstice. Others were told only in the evening or during sunset. This is because those stories related to specific moments when they held spiritual power relative to the motion of the universe—yet another example of the importance of relationships in Indigenous cultures. Unifying metaphor with a time of year or day placed it into an understandable context, merging meaning with the interaction and flow of imagery.

Indigenous languages, unlike the binary Euro-American languages, flow like a breeze moving through the forest. As Margaret Kovach explains in her book *Indigenous Methodologies*: "Skilled orators, then and now, can imbue energy through word choice and allow listeners to walk inside the story to find their own teachings. With the listener's involvement, the insight gained from the story is a highly particular and relevant form of knowledge exchange."

Picture hundreds of years ago, as the sun is heading toward the western horizon, a group of people gather around a storyteller in a clearing with longhouses, gardens encircling the community and food warmed over a fire in front of each house. The tall trees reach toward the sky full of songbirds, and the crickets are starting to pulsate sounds. The storyteller begins to speak.

The following is a shortened version of the story about the creation of the Haudenosaunee League. The challenge is to see the metaphoric flow of each personality's relationship to the whole.

Metaphor Through the Native Perspective

One of the Iroquois legends relates to the forming of the Haudenosaunee League. Four tribes wanted to unite with the Onondaga in a confederacy, an idea proposed by Deganawidah (the Peacemaker) from the Wendat Confederacy and Hayo'wetha (more commonly known as Hiawatha).

They were unsuccessful until they asked Jigonsaseh of the Erie or Neutral Nation, who lived near Niagara Falls, to join the effort, because she was known for her hospitality. No matter who was passing by or in conflict, warriors were invited into her home, fed, and allowed to rest. Enemies ate and rested peacefully side by side. She did not allow weapons inside. This part of the legend unites feminine energy and its far-sighted relationship-orientation with the masculine. Her role is often omitted in Euro-American versions of the story.

In the story, Onondaga leader Tadodaho had "snakes in his hair" that made him difficult to approach. But he allowed Jigonsaseh to approach him and remove the snakes.

It would be easy to misinterpret the symbolism of the snakes. But as discussed in the Linguistics chapter, snakes do not represent a denigration in Native cultures. One must look at the nature of snakes to understand that part of the metaphor. Snakes are isolates, as was Tadodaho. Once Jigonsaseh removed the snakes, Tadodaho's personality shifted, and he became more connected, communal, and cooperative.

This reflects how the feminine side was able to soften resistance, leading to peace and the formation of the League. And it is an example of feminine masculine balance.

Today, the confederacy still meets on the Onondaga Reservation, and the council leader is still known as Tadodaho.

An Iroquois Story of Relationship: The Three Sisters

> *Being among the sisters provides a visible manifestation of what a community can become when its members understand and share their gifts.*
> —Robin Wall Kimmerer, *Braiding Sweetgrass*

The following is a condensed version of the Three Sisters myth based on a story provided by a Mohawk Elder in *Preserving a Past, Providing a Future* (Ganondagan Seneca Art and Culture Center). The Cherokee version is different, but the metaphors provide similar relationship insights. The story goes like this:

When the daughter of Sky Woman, a common figure in the Iroquois creation stories, passed away, she was buried in the dirt that a little muskrat had brought up from the bottom of the water to cover the earth. From that soil grew the Three Sisters. The oldest sister, representing corn, stood tall, in a "pale green shawl … with yellow hair that tossed around in the breeze." She had to constantly watch her younger sister so she would not roam away. The younger sister, representing beans, wore a frock of bright yellow. A third sister, representing squash, was the youngest and crawled along the ground dressed only in green. The sisters never left each other's side.

One day, a little boy strolled into the field occupied by the three sisters. He walked with determination. The boy already had a sense of communicating with the earth and the animals around him. The Three Sisters were curious about him as they watched him and wondered where he went at night. Late in that summer, the youngest of the Three Sisters disappeared. The other two sisters mourned for her until the fall.

After a while, the boy appeared again. He sat by a nearby stream gathering reeds to make arrow shafts. They watched as the boy left. His moccasin tracks disappeared out of the clearing into the forest. That night the second sister left, the one who always wanted to run away. She left no trail and may have used the boy's moccasin tracks to conceal her direction.

The older sister stood, sad and alone. As the weeks passed, the days grew shorter, the nights colder, her shawl shriveled, and her hair faded and grew tangled in the wind.

One day, at harvest time, the boy heard the sorrowful calls of the older sister. He followed the sound of her mourning and gathered her up, taking her back home. There the two sisters greeted her. The three worked through the winter to provide for the little boy combining their different nutritional qualities.

In the Indigenous mythologies, there is an unbroken flow between the world defined by the five senses and the spirit world. This is reflected in the story as each of the three sisters disappears and reappears elsewhere. In the Native whole brain thought process, this does not pose an issue, but it may for the Western mind, which defines things more concretely. This also illustrates how Native mythology is more layered than it first appears.

The story interacts with the audience. Native Americans grew up in a culture listening to such orations from a storyteller, surrounded by nature. Imagine how that changed the way they saw relationships to that natural world. Story and metaphor strengthened the psychological and emotional sense of relationship. Out of that psyche emerged the many Native contributions we still use today.

Story Variations

The story of *Onenha, The Corn,* serves as a bridge connecting Native culture to its material contributions. It is from the Tuscarora Iroquois tradition and follows two intertwined metaphorical themes: gardening and the Circle of Life.

This story takes place in the eastern woodland area, where most Native peoples were agriculturists who grew corn, beans, and squash as well as sunflower seeds, and more. When people traveled, they sometimes dropped seeds on the trail.

There was an old man who enjoyed spending time walking through the forests listening to the life all around him. When he saw seeds on the ground, he picked them up and told them he would take care of them.

One day, when he was far from home, he suddenly became ill, too ill to travel further. It was getting late, and chilly weather was approaching. The forest provided leaves and other natural materials that he gathered to build a tiny shelter. He rested, but he grew worse. After four days, he began to hear women's voices discussing how to help him. He looked out from under his robe covering but no one was there.

That fourth night, he had a dream about a beautiful woman whose voice sounded like the singing wind among corn stalks. She told him, "On the trails, you saw my sisters and me [corn, beans, and squash seeds], and you took care of us. That is why we have come to help you." He was instructed to make a little cup and place it where it could catch rainwater. "Drink it. It is a medicine that will cure you." In the dream, she foretold a time when he would hear her and her sisters singing in the fields. The first time would be when the seeds sprout; the second, when they sing and dance in thanksgiving; the third, before the second hoeing; and the fourth, when the corn is ready for harvest. She told him to take the songs to his people.

If they sang them in future growing seasons, and danced as the corn people danced, they would always provide the people with what they need. This became known as the Corn Dance.

Clearly, corn was more than a simple crop, as Maxidiwiac (Buffalo Bird Woman) of the Hidatsa community explained: "We cared for our corn in those days as we care for our children; for we Indian people loved our gardens, just as a mother loves her children; and we thought that our growing corn liked to hear us sing, just as children like to hear their mother sing to them" (Caduto, Michael J. and Bruchac, 1–4).

The Teachings of the *Diné* (Navajo) Creation Story

Imagine a group of people of all ages gathering around a storyteller in late afternoon, as the sun is setting in the west. This time the group is in a desert landscape, surrounded by mountains with piñon and pine vegetation. Gigantic stone monoliths tower toward the sky with huge stone "window rock" formations nearby. A warm breeze flows through the circle of people surrounding the storyteller.

The Navajo (Diné) creation story unfolds in four layers out of four worlds. In the first, far below the world of today, the masculine and feminine are represented by six beings. The First

Man is the son of Night and the Blue Sky over the sunset; First Woman, the daughter of Day Break and the Yellow Sky of the sunset. *Begochiddy*, who was the child of the Sun, was both man and woman, and had blue eyes and golden hair. There were no mountains in this first world, so Begochiddy made four mountains, which were white to the east, yellow to the west, black to the north, and blue to the south. (Color meanings varied among tribes.)

As time passed, the people moved to a second, third, and fourth world, where they received instructions on how to maintain a proper relationship with all that had been added.

> When Coyote, the human beings, and the others reach the Fourth World, Begochiddy tells the human beings how to live right, to care for the plants and to give thanks, for the Fourth World, our world of today, can also be destroyed by human beings.
> —Michael J. Caduto and Joseph Bruchac, *Keepers of the Earth: Native American Stories and Environmental Activities for Children*

The Meanings in Metaphor

The stories above contain nuances that cannot be translated into English. What is important is to see that they are about interconnecting relationships and to understand the flow of meaning.

Although the Onondaga and *Diné* stories (from opposite ends of the continent and contrasting environments) appear different, the metaphors of the stories merge. For example, both contain feminine and masculine energy, which are critical aspects of cultural survival.

Metaphors make narratives personal. Imagine a 10-year-old girl sitting beside an eighty-year-old Elder, listening to one of the stories above. How might the images differ in their minds? Listeners' understanding grew over time, making the story a deepening intellectual pursuit. As the listeners grew older, their understanding also grew.

Years ago, I attended a symposium at Lakehead University in Thunder Bay, Ontario. It included educators from around the country. During one of the sessions, a debate developed spontaneously over how to interpret the writings of Joseph Campbell, Professor Emeritus of World Mythologies at Sarah Lawrence College.

Two female professors from Yale University were Campbell enthusiasts.

An Apache woman from the University of Arizona disagreed with the women from Yale and their praise of Campbell, arguing that understanding metaphor is a personal process. She believed it was a cultural imposition for Joseph Campbell to interpret the world's metaphorical writings through a single methodology. What he provided was simply his own metaphorical process. She argued you defeat the purpose of metaphor when you rely on a scholar's analysis, because interpreting metaphor is about personal growth and personal maturation. It is a process, not a result. Learning that makes you grow, not in knowledge, but in a sense of "knowing."

It's important to put the opposing arguments in perspective.

The difference in intellectual viewpoints between the nation-state and the tribal is profound.

The women from Yale reflected a culture that teaches an outside-in process. The teacher offers insight to the students who are later tested for their understanding of the class offerings. In the modern world, the concrete often replaces metaphor. They therefore assumed Campbell's interpretation of metaphors was the correct one. But, as previously illustrated, Native stories were created to foster an unfolding understanding. A binary mindset does not immediately recognize the many shades of meaning that characterized Native metaphor.

The Apache woman embodied her traditional values of an inside-out process that allows a sense of *a priori* intellectual growth on the part of the listener. Metaphor is an important part of that process. As one ages and gains life experience, those experiences and the *a priori* cultural values merge into intellectual growth.

The meanings behind Native American stories are for each individual to discover at various points in their lives. If someone else interprets them for you, it defeats the purpose of metaphor and undermines this section of the book, which focuses on understanding the Indigenous thought process.

Metaphoric Definitions Reflect Different Value Systems

The idea of good and evil did not exist in the American hemisphere at the time these stories were shared through oral tradition. Good vs. evil first entered this part of the world with Cristobel Colon (Christopher Columbus). Try to view these Indigenous stories as a process of establishing sustainability through balance and harmony. Do not let "good vs. evil" block your understanding.

"Witch" and "evil" are two terms that often slip into English translations of Native stories told in the oral tradition. Both are Euro-American concepts. Indigenous mythologies include metaphors representing negative energy, but in the Native ethos, negative energies express imbalance rather than evil.

The Power of Memory in Oral Tradition

In thinking about the Indigenous oral tradition, I am reminded of the incident that occurred when a Norse woman, at her home around a thousand years ago, encountered an Indigenous girl in what is today northeastern Canada. The woman introduced herself and explained what she was doing. When she was through talking, the Native girl repeated exactly what the woman had said in the Norse language with an identical accent. The girl had never been around Norse people before. This is an example of the amazing memorization skills developed by those who listened to the stories that passed through the generations.

Another Native story that illustrates the concepts presented in this chapter is the Siouan Red Horn Cycles. The challenge for us is to try to see these myths as Indigenous peoples did hundreds of years ago. Notice where tensions in the story occur and how they are reconciled.

Metaphor Captured Complexities in Context

As we move onto stories about the workings of the universe, the metaphors tend to become more complex and challenging to understand. The Red Horn stories are good examples. Red Horn was a spiritual force, a metaphorical individual who changed physically to fit each story's transforming relationships. Many of the stories were told only at specific times, containing layered meanings we might miss.

The Siouan Red Horn Cycles (The Son of Earth Maker)

The "Red Horn" stories were told by many peoples, from the Winnebago in Wisconsin to the Quapaw in Arkansas. The rich array of Red Horn stories has been published in several volumes, but many remain unpublished and are passed down orally. The central figure of the stories, Red Horn, exists simultaneously as both an individual and a spirit. Red Horn "shape shifts" back and forth but is still identifiable if you follow the flow. In the traditional Indigenous mind, energy flows like a river from the material world to the world of the spirit, as though they are one.

There are many stories, some of which are quite lengthy, partly because of the metamorphosing qualities of Red Horn. Translating these stories into English, along with the required cultural leap, makes fully capturing the metaphors' meanings a challenge.

One Winnebago myth identifies Red Horn as a star. In this version of the story, ten brothers live together in a longhouse. By dancing all night and performing hunting rites, the brothers are able to attract wives. The second oldest brother, Hena, is jealous because his younger brother "Wears Faces on His Ears" (Red Horn) attracts the fattest woman. Hena persuades some of the other brothers to join him in a plot to rid themselves of Wears Faces. They encourage him to visit the lodge of a beautiful woman who is *wakcexi,* a water spirit. She lures him to the back of her lodge where he falls through a trap door into the underworld and becomes a captive of *wakcexi sisik*, bad water spirits. Wears Faces breaks free of his bindings and escapes. He then takes revenge on his brothers by turning them into foxes and coyotes. Two brothers who had remained loyal to Wears Faces become stars in the heavens.

There is debate among scholars about Red Horn's transformation into a star. In 1945, after many years of research, Paul Radin suggested Red Horn had become known to the Hocagara (Winnebago) as Wiragosge Xetera, the Morning Star. He adjusted that conclusion several times until 1954, when he settled on Red Horn becoming the Evening Star. The change from Morning to Evening star may seem insignificant, but it shifted all the metaphorical relationships and meanings of the myth.

This illustrates the challenge of seeing through the Native eye, which is anchored in both the laws of physics and a rich metaphorical, mythological tradition. Even those like Radin, who dedicated his life to the field of anthropology with significant focus on the Winnebago and Anishinaabeg, faced this challenge.

In looking at the flow of energy in the Red Horn story, there is an incredible amount of transformation—both physical and internal. In fact, every character goes through transformation. When Red Horn is tricked into going to the water spirit's lodge, water becomes part of the story. This is a clue about what is happening. Water in these mythologies is often symbolic of transformation as we saw in the water serpents in the kiva bowl discussed in the previous chapter. When he falls through the trap door, he is physically transformed into a captive in the underworld. There he uses a brand of fire against the bad water spirits, fire possibly representing assertiveness and passion. In the ancient Winnebago mind, does this equate to facing his own demons? It's important to remember that each listener relates to the story differently, depending on their age and experiences.

Red Horn's journey is transformative: from being manipulated by his brothers, to being tempted by a beautiful water spirit, to his transformation in the underworld, to the transformation of the water spirit *wakcexi*, to transforming both his jealous and supportive brothers when he returns, and finally transforming again to a star in the heavens. The story is about a soul's transformation. It's a journey for all of us, which the Lakota call your *Zuya* or life's journey.

The Stability of Whole Brain Development

The dualistic energy of the universe flows like a river, and Indigenous metaphors weave through it. Metaphor unites the left and right brain functions as the voice of the storyteller is transformed into images in our minds. The listeners' thought process shifts to a unification of the feminine and masculine, a movement in harmony.

Native interpretations of story are individualized, yet they emanate out of a common anchor point: the physics of nature. The Native oral tradition helps ensure sustainability by reconciling the constant state of tension embedded in the dualistic nature of the universe. Indigenous oration introduces and reconciles those tensions. The resulting knowledge is an unfolding process, not an end result.

Native peoples were whole brain thinkers. Their stories reflected a flow of energy and understanding and focused on metaphorical forms moving in a sense of wholeness. The result was stable cultures that survived for thousands of years.

CHAPTER 8

NATIVE SPIRITUALITY

Spirituality was at the core of all Native American cultures. It was fundamental and permeated everything. It was and is experiential, evolving over a lifetime in community. It encourages personal growth through spiritual self-discovery within the oneness of all things. Though there is a deep understanding of the natural forces in the universe, Native spiritual growth is individualized and cannot be put into a written or ministered paradigm.

In discussing Native spirituality, I speak only for myself, coming from my personal understanding and growth on that lifelong path. I am not Native, and I do not speak for Native peoples.

Because of my non-Indigenous urban background, my understandings are still young; even in my eighties, my wisdom is not that of a Native-born Elder. In the ancient traditions, empowering oneself is essential in order to mature. The statement by John Trudell, an Isanti Dakota, gives an example of how that level of inclusivity may look in today's stressed Indigenous world: "No matter what they ever do to us, we must always act for the love of our people and the earth. We must not react out of hatred against those who have no sense."

It's easy for the Western mind to project itself into Indigenous spirituality, but that can easily go astray. If you have ever played the "telephone" game where each person whispers a phrase to the next, you've learned that by the time it gets to the last person, the phrase is distorted. That is one of the most challenging obstacles in the fields of historiography and anthropology. The challenge intensifies when attempting to understand and communicate the ethos of a vastly different culture, particularly its spirituality.

Native spirituality emphasizes the rhythmic nature of the universe in the sense that each one of us is part of the whole. It is well-organized and has only one requirement: it must not infringe upon the community's vision or anyone's personal experiences with spiritual forces. Indigenous rituals are governed by the principle that each individual has a personal experience with the spirit world.

I took my 12-year-old stepdaughter to an informal talk given by a Lakota friend, Archie Fire Lame Deer. He spoke for about two hours. It is traditional for Native speakers to use whole brain communication. Often when they speak, a linear-binary thinker may wonder, "Where is he going with this? He's all over the map!" In about the last ten to 15 minutes of his talk, it was like the pieces of a puzzle falling into place. The picture created by those pieces was clear. What appeared to be rambling all over the place in the linear-binary Euro-American thought process, was really bits of pieces of an interconnected whole, typical of Native oratory. What was surprising was that, as we got in the car, my stepdaughter could not stop talking about the wonder she had felt listening to Archie Fire Lame Deer talk. Ever try to hold a 12-year-old's attention for any length of time?

Everything in traditional Native culture is soul-felt, and this was no exception.

A Deep Connection to Nature

> *The one who plants trees, knowing that he will never sit in their shade, has at least started to understand the meaning of life.*
>
> —Rabindranath Tagore

Another friend, spiritual leader Godfrey Chipps, lived five miles outside Wanblee on the Pine Ridge Oglala Lakota (Sioux) Reservation. Eagle Nest Butte is a huge, beautiful formation outside Wanblee, and it is very important to the Native community. Although it was on the reservation, Euro-Americans owned it. That ownership decision had been made by the Federal Government's Bureau of Indian Affairs in conjunction with an earlier tribal council.

Although they were already using it for spiritual practices, my friend wanted to buy the butte to protect it for future use. To raise funds for that purchase, he created a nonprofit corporation and, cleverly, called it Organized Religion. Ironically, the name was accepted because there was no other legally registered organization with that name in the United States.

On the surface, that appears very contradictory. However, Native spirituality is highly organized both conceptually and structurally, while simultaneously encouraging a great deal of independence and interaction. Although his effort failed, it came out of a sincere spiritual foundation.

Native spirituality includes the seen and unseen—that which incorporates the five senses and that which is beyond them. All that is natural is equal; humans are not "above." I have witnessed thankful tears in the eyes of a Polacca woman when discussing gathering clay for her pottery, and a Lakota medicine person being moved to tears while gathering the healing plant Pejuta Skan for medicinal purposes. There are many other examples of Indigenous peoples shedding tears for their land, including the Choctaws who cried as they were driven from their homeland. Those tears reflect the deep Indigenous connection of being one with the land.

Spirituality vs. Superstition

To understand Native spirituality, you must experience it.

Instruction, interpretations, and definitions are poor substitutes. There was no salvation, no heaven, no hell, no evil. Children were nurtured into thoughtful, responsible adulthood with a strong sense of self-identity, eliminating the need for such outside-in concepts. It was intertwined with a spirituality that was a personal, experiential process leading to greater growth and understanding. Organized religion differs by focusing on institutional, top-down instruction in contrast to engagement in personal growth, often fostered by ceremony. Any Indigenous instruction received was to help guide one's personal process on that journey toward greater knowing, rather than administering an institutional belief system.

Indigenous spirituality is about more than belief. It is an interaction with the spiritual forces of which we are a part. It is a relationship, and there are rules of propriety in the interaction just as there are in all relationships.

To explain it academically, we can say it is the reconciliation of duality that brings about sustainability within oneself. But that description fails to capture the experience of spirituality, and spiritual reality must be experienced to be fully understood. That is why I included a qualifier at the beginning of this chapter.

I have read highly respected authors who imply that Indigenous spirituality is superstition. Actual experience falsifies that notion, exposing a cultural bias and narrow view. Spiritual forces are real, just as real as the natural world, which has directly connected Native Americans to the spiritual for thousands of years. And it leads us to accept those spiritual forces without need for explanation.

There are specific ceremonies that connect the consciousness of an individual to the spirit world, but that connection is not limited to those ceremonies. For example, in the 19th century and before, death songs were common. The Blackfoot song I mentioned in the Preface was sung by an individual who, even in death, maintained a deep connection to all life and its flow into the spirit world. People who have touched that spirit in ceremony do not fear death.

The written word is incapable of touching Native spirituality because it is participatory. Without that interaction you cannot have the experience. And without that experience, you cannot understand what it is. In other words, the only way to understand chocolate is to taste it.

Ceremonial Rules of Spirituality

There are rules of conduct in Indigenous spiritual ceremonies. For those rules of conduct, there is one litmus test: does the conduct enhance the growth of spiritual connection, of personal consciousness to the spirit world, and does it enhance understanding of those spiritual relationships?

There is no intermediary between the individual and spiritual understanding as there is in the Abrahamic religions—no churches, mosques, or synagogues, no priests, no liturgy. There is only the individual's relationship within the spiritual context of ritual, the context of Native ceremony from which personal growth emerges. The stages of the journey toward these ceremonies are actually a process of maturity. An individual's personal growth is almost synonymous with one's spiritual growth and the health of community.

> *This is my simple religion.*
> *No need for temples; No need for complicated philosophy. Your own mind, your own heart is the temple; Your philosophy is simple kindness.*
> —14th Dalai Lama

Indigenous spirituality mitigates the ego and connects the heart and soul to the community—the universe. The sun is Father, and the earth is Mother. As the energy of the sun touches the earth, all life emerges. The stars are incorporated into Indigenous metaphor in oral tradition and story, creating deep interpersonal relationships between the tribal community and that sense of unity with the whole of the universe.

That spirituality is grounded in egalitarianism, fully acknowledging birth, life, and death as equal partners in sustainability. Ceremony guides the individual through that growth process. Ceremony weaves in the death of ignorance and immaturity, making room for the birth of expansive new life in the Native mind and soul. Ceremony addresses the struggles, the release from those struggles, and the ecstasy of life, which eventually evolves into the wisdom of the Elders. And that wisdom comes full circle back into traditional community. That is tribalism at its core.

For forty years, I have attended and participated in Lakota Sundances, Inipi, and other Indigenous ceremonies. As a non-Native, I can only write from my own perspective, and it is important to remember that I did not grow up in an Indigenous community. I approach this passion of mine with humility. But what I see from that perspective is a people of deep spiritual sophistication and wisdom.

I was in my early forties when I touched my own spirituality during a Lakota ceremony, experiencing the death of a part of myself to make room for the growth of a deeper understanding of "self." Each step fostered a growth toward greater maturity and inner strength. Each ceremony deepened my ability to feel, to be compassionate, and to love. My experiences and relationships with traditional people showed me American history in a very different light than what I had learned in school. No one talked to me about that history. But the experience gave me a knowing about it that cannot be learned in a classroom.

Because of my experiences with Indigenous communities over that forty plus years, I believe most books and classrooms miss the reality of Indigenous cultures; miss the reality of the Indigenous thought process. I now see much of what I read was projection of a Euro-American mentality that just does not fit.

Taking Personal Responsibility

In Native spirituality, the individual decides to act and asks for support from the spirit world. It is not about asking those spiritual powers to solve a problem or to take care of a serious situation. There is no plea for help, because if you see the universe as all one, you are part of that oneness. There is no institutional intermediary. It is like deciding to solve a family problem and asking for support. It is that sense of universal oneness, where the universe is that family: Mother Earth and Father Sun.

One of the ceremonies designed to promote healing and personal growth is the Sundance. Sundancers do not dance for themselves. Their dance is always for the well-being of others, be it a person or any part of the natural world. They decide which actions to take to provide that spiritual help. Participation in the Sundance demands a strenuous commitment that involves physical sacrifice and endurance.

The drum—heartbeat of Mother Earth—song, and dance, is about connecting the consciousness to the spiritual. That connection is always present, but the dance focuses on asking for support within that relationship to the spirit world. That level of sincerity on the part of the dancers connects everyone into a oneness of intention.

I will never forget a Sundance on the Rosebud Lakota Reservation several years ago. On the first of the four-day ceremony, I noticed a man dancing whose eyes never left the tree in the center of the circle. That ceremonial tree has deep spiritual meaning to the dancers.

On the third day, as he continued to dance while looking at the tree, his rhythm resembled the movement of a buffalo. I was captivated by that feeling that emanated from him. I found out during that time that his three-year-old nephew had swallowed the contents of a bottle of highly toxic cleaning fluid. He was in the hospital. Doctors gave the family no hope for his recovery. At the end of the fourth (and last) day, I saw that man by the tree with one hand on the trunk and his head bowed. As he turned around and walked out of the Sundance circle, I saw he was holding the little boy, who was looking around curiously, as though nothing had happened. In that moment, I emotionally felt that oneness. My understanding of the word "power" was shifting to something very different from status, wealth, influence, and force.

This exemplifies the unexplainable aspect of spirituality found in the relationship between the known and the unknown.

One year at the Sundance, I was asked to be on "security." On the second day, between dance cycles, a man charged the dancers' rest area with a knife. Several of the Sundance leaders intercepted him and carried him struggling and screaming to an area behind some tipis. They placed him on the ground and began to talk to him in calm voices. The distressed man finally began to relax. I returned to my station and saw him later that day under the arbor watching the dance as though the incident had not occurred. I do not know what the Sundance leaders did to help him, but he was perfectly calm the following two days as well. One of the leaders who had carried him out told me that spiritual forces at the Sundance had triggered subconscious memories of an abusive childhood leading to what appeared to be a psychotic break. If he had been in any other environment, the police probably would have arrested or hospitalized him.

Quantum Spirituality

Growing up in the city gave me no context through which to understand my experiences in the Native spiritual world. But those experiences motivated me to look deeper.

At first, I saw quantum physics as the only pathway to explaining the unknown and what I had personally experienced in the Native culture.

Physicists Max Planck and Niels Bohr, considered the fathers of quantum physics, developed the theory that radiant energy is made up of particle-like components known as "quanta." The theory helped resolve earlier mysterious natural phenomena such as the nature of light absorption on the atomic level. In 1918, Planck won the Nobel Prize in physics for his work in radiation.

German-born Albert Einstein is perhaps the best-known theoretical physicist. He created the Theory of Special and General Relativity and worked on Quantum Theory, which studies the smallest particles in the universe, such as subatomic particles, and neutrinos. I thought that analysis of the smallest of the physical world would provide the answer to what I experienced. I read *Blackfoot Physics* by University of Liverpool physicist F. David Peat, who had attended a Sundance in Alberta, Canada. That motivated him into further studies of Indigenous ceremony and the unexplainable. I also read a book by Fred A. Wolf, Ph.D., physicist and National Book Award winner for *Taking the Quantum Leap: The New Physics for Nonscientists*. Wolf had attended ceremonies on the Pine Ridge Reservation and had experiences he was also unable to explain.

Although Harvard University's Department of Physics does not seem to be currently approaching the issue of Indigenous knowledge, years ago I traveled to St. Louis, Missouri, to hear a talk by Harvard Physicist Lisa Randall at Washington University. I had studied her book *Warped Passages: Unraveling the Mysteries of the Universe's Hidden Dimensions* and was captivated by her discussion of extra dimensions and particle physics. Her talk was as intellectual as one would expect, and I came away with a respect for the depth of her research, but also a deeper understanding of the universe's remaining mysteries. I felt reconciled by the fact of not needing to understand all that I had experienced in Native American communities. It was liberating to realize I didn't have to explain experiences. I simply had to be open to them.

Particle physics experiments are one of science's most recent attempts to solve the mysteries of the universe, and yet with the endless billions of dollars and efforts of brilliant scientists dedicated to this endeavor, the mystery remains. So does my curiosity about what I have experienced in Native spirituality.

All these attempts at understanding have taught me that I do not need explanations. I just need to experience life as it is, at least for now. The unexplainable will remain unexplainable, and the Native world of spirituality will continue to be both a mystery and a great gift of experience.

What Is Power?

The traditional Native concept of power is very different from our Western view, and describing it is difficult.

As I have said in other parts of this book, the Euro-American view is defined by material acquisition and leverage. Now consider an Indigenous definition that comes from contact with the spirit world.

Having spiritual experiences is an integral part of Native life. These experiences are powerful and transformative, yet they have a different kind of "power" that is difficult to explain in Euro-American cultural terms.

Maybe this is why metaphor was so valued in Native culture: it provided a way to discuss the unexplainable. For example, imagine a being made of light and electricity. It is unlike anything you have seen before. It looks different, moves differently, can communicate without words, and can transform itself and you. This metaphor describes a concept not meant to be taken literally.

How does it change your definition of power?

Now consider the medicine person who lives in a small hundred-year-old two-room house on the reservation. I have known such people. They are not stoic. They simply understand what true power is—the power that exists in the spirit world. And they feel no need for acquisition because they see no connection between true power and materialism.

Much of the following comes from my experience of spirituality in the Lakota, Nakota, and Dakota cultures. The foundational understandings, however, are present in Indigenous cultures coast-to-coast. From the following descriptions, one can extrapolate the multicultural levels of spiritual understanding.

The Dance of Life

> *The circle of life for the Lakota and Dakota has always been both simple and complex. Prayer, ritual, dance, and music were part of the dance of life*

> *... and .... a way to keep the history of the people alive.*
> "Oceti Sakowin – The People of the Seven Council Fires," PBS, 9/8/2007.

In Indigenous culture, dancing is spiritual. Tribal members often dance ceremonially to the rhythms for hours. While common sense might suggest the dancers would become exhausted, they actually gain strength and eventually become recharged through the process. Indigenous spiritual dance is about sharing strength and uniting consciousness with the cosmos. The drum is the heartbeat of Mother Earth and of the thunder beings. The rhythms and movement are transformative, even for observers, unifying the rhythmic flow of the dancers with the universe. And, in that struggle between energy and exhaustion, one finds beauty.

Today, traditional dance is not frozen in the past. Yet the essential transformative property remains unchanged: through that struggle between energy and exhaustion, one finds not a static universe, but a timeless reality in constant motion.

For Native Americans, life is spirituality in motion. If the Western mind can begin to connect with these rhythms, one can begin to feel the essence of tribalism. The challenge is profound, as it requires a significant leap for the Western psyche and an open mind regarding the range of human potential.

Significant Numbers

In Indigenous North America, there are numbers that represent spiritual forces in the universe.

The number four represents the energies coming out of what

Euro-Americans would call directions. The traditional Indigenous mind thinks of those four directions as spiritual powers emanating out of the universe. Numbers five and six are Mother Earth and Father Sun, below and above us. And the seventh, in the center, is personal (you and me), as each of us is a part of the whole. In Native spirituality, each person chooses to act and then seeks spiritual support. In contrast, prayer in the Abrahamic religions is more passive, asking for divine help and guidance.

Four times seven equals twenty-eight, which is also a significant number, as is eleven, the sum of seven and four. In ancient times, the tipi lodge poles often numbered twenty-eight. Even today, some tipis still feature twenty-eight poles. The numbers reflect the fact that the spiritual lived in the consciousness of the people.

The organizational structure of the Oceti Sakowin (People of the Seven Council Fires) was based on the spiritual number seven. For example, there are four Dakota groupings, two Nakota groupings, and one Lakota people, which is further subdivided into seven groups.

The Lakota year was based on that numbering system. For example, the calendar was lunar, consisting of 13 months, each with 28 days.

The Rite of Adoption

Lakota *tiyospayes* (lineages/bands) are matrilineal. An individual becomes a member by birth, marriage, or adoption. One of the Lakota rites is the *Hunkakaga* (adoption) ceremony. Over 40 years ago, I was adopted by the Dion family at Lake Andes on the Ihanktonwah Nakota/Dakota Reservation. My understanding

My Adopted Family: I am on the left with my adopted family. Neulin Dion is in the center and his wife, Diane, is holding the baby.

of Native spirituality grew immensely through that adoptive relationship. It was not just through language. I learned a lot about Indigenous people through their body language as well as their gentle and loving care.

My experience was a very spiritual process. When you are adopted into a tribal family, you are treated respectfully as a family member. You are referred to by relationship names, such as "younger brother" or "nephew." It took time to get used to the fact that proper names are seldom used in traditional communities.

One year, I traveled to a Sundance ceremony, and as I walked near the ceremonial circle, I heard someone call out "Uncle!" I kept walking because I did not hear my proper name. Then I suddenly realized I was no longer in the Euro-American world. I turned around to be greeted by one of my adopted nephews.

As reflected in this chapter, the "relationship" was all-encompassing. From the spirit world to the surrounding flora and fauna, to our humanity—both inter- and intra-tribal—we were all Mitakuya Oyasin; we were all together in oneness. This is why, before 1492, inter-tribal conflict was mitigated by that culture of "oneness."

The Special Role of Women

"Women are the backbone of the nation," is a phrase frequently stated by tribal people.

Women are the educators of the people and nurturers of the home. The grandmothers were the educators of the young. Before the colonial period, women's roles were in separate but equal spheres with men. The ancient wisdom and wellspring of knowledge came from both the grandmothers and grandfathers.

Origins of Spiritual Consciousness

Every tribe has its own origin story. The Lakota version recounts the tale of Ptehincela Ska Win (White Buffalo Calf Woman). The story begins at a period in their tribal history when food was scarce. Nature was not providing for the needs of the community. Two men were out hunting for food. They had been out for four days (a sacred number) without success. Suddenly, from far off in the distance, a cloud approached them very rapidly. It suddenly disappeared and a beautiful woman stood before them. One of the men felt desire for her. A cloud descended over him and then lifted, exposing his skeleton. Ptehincela Ska Win turned to the other man and told him to return to his people and tell them she would come in four days to give them something that would secure their future. He returned to his people and shared his experiences. They set up a huge council tipi for her arrival.

On the designated day, she appeared at sunrise on the eastern horizon carrying a bundle. She entered the council tipi and moved in a sunwise direction, stopping halfway around. There, she opened the bundle and explained its sacred contents. This was a gift from the Creator. In the bundle was the Canumpa (a sacred pipe). She also gave them four ceremonies and explained that three more would come later. As she left, she turned into a buffalo calf—first black, then red, then yellow, then white (colors representing the "directional" spiritual powers)—and disappeared over the northern horizon. That is how the Lakota got their sacred Canumpa.

Story Variations

One year, at the Rosebud Lakota Reservation, some of us were invited to an outdoor dinner. An Elder woman told the Ptehíŋčala Ska Wiŋ legend. She added something interesting that I had never heard before, and since she was an Elder and a woman, it resonated with me. When she reached the part where the two men first came upon White Buffalo Calf Woman, and the cloud descended over one man, she diverted away from the story I had heard before. She said the man had fallen instantly in love with Ptehíŋčala Ska Wiŋ, and that they lived a long time in a loving relationship until he died at an old age. That lifetime in the consciousness of the other man lasted only a few seconds. And that was why, when the cloud lifted, the skeleton was all that remained of his hunting partner.

The addition of love between the man and Ptehíŋčala Ska Wiŋ makes a beautiful tapestry woven with the threads of metaphor, giving their relationship a deeper meaning. Indigenous languages emphasize relationships in their interactions, offering a perspective that sees the whole of humanity through the lens of relationship. The love of the man for Ptehíŋčala Ska Wiŋ added a powerful and more complete meaning: that love is the foundation of spirituality.

This illustrates that women told the feminine version of a story, and men told the masculine version, representing their distinct roles. Today, with so many Native Americans not living on reservations, they often do not hear both versions of a story as they once did in a community. The two versions contain nuanced differences, but together they form a union between the masculine and the feminine.

One mystery in the story is the element of time and why a lifetime for one man was seconds for the other. It made me think of Albert Einstein's theory of General Relativity. At the speed of light, there is no dimension of time. When astronauts went to the moon in 1969, it was calculated that at the speed they had traveled, they gained five minutes on their lifetime.

As an aside, the Jesuits often manipulated Indigenous spirituality to fit Christian constructs. This was sometimes reflected in more contemporary versions of ancient stories that were once told in a close-knit community setting, where masculine and feminine had equal influence. As more Native Americans leave the reservations, that unification is less available, and teaching the importance of masculine and feminine equality becomes more challenging.

Ptehíŋčala Ska Wiŋ's bundle is still housed on the Cheyenne River Reservation. Its guardians, the Arvol Looking Horse family, have protected it for nineteen generations. A Sundance is performed there every year, and the bundle is ceremonially opened periodically.

The Ptehíŋčala Ska Wiŋ story is considered the origin of the people's spiritual consciousness. It renewed the covenant between the creator and the people and gave them changeless spiritual laws.

The Power of the Indigenous Oral Tradition

Native languages have words that express life values. For example, the Lakota words *Wizanni* and *Wicozani* refer to health and happiness on all levels of our humanity and define a part of life's path. Those words also encompass one's spirituality in daily life.

There is a fluidity in metaphor, and as previously discussed, the stories often have different versions, but the deeper meanings remain consistent. The key to Indigenous oral history is to look deeper into the meanings of the interactive relationships. Native storytelling takes the human mind and spirit deeper into those relationships and is an example of "power" being spiritual, not physical or political.

Canumpa: The Sacred Pipe

One of the Lakota ceremonies is the *Canumpa* (sacred pipe) ceremony. These pipes have been ceremonially connected to the power of the original pipe brought by Ptehíŋčala Ska Wiŋ.

A sacred pipe is stored in two pieces: the stem, and the pipe bowl. Metaphorically, attaching the bowl to the stem represents a unification of the feminine and the masculine, of balance and harmony. The ceremonial smoke and the accompanying drumbeat and songs send a message into the atmosphere that connects one's consciousness to the spirit world. In my experience, tobacco and other plant materials are placed into the pipe bowl. I want to clarify that NO hallucinogens are put into a pipe bowl in Indigenous tradition. Such falsehoods are a disservice to the nation's Indigenous communities.

Euro-American Impact on Native Spirituality

The systematic attempts to destroy Native spirituality took many forms. The United States disregarded Native American rights to the land, drove them from their homelands, forced Christianity on them, confined them to reservations where they starved, forced their children into inhumane boarding schools to interrupt their understanding of their own culture, and took a role in their governance.

Today, more than 70% of Native Americans do not live on reservations, and many both off and on reservations are disconnected from their heritage. For example, while in a Jesuit Mission Museum on a Lakota reservation, I asked a young man who worked there a question about a Canumpa in the collection. He did not know the term Canumpa or its cultural importance. I had to show it to him before he even knew what I was talking about.

The disconnect from their culture has confused Native children's identity. Due to that sense of anomie, youth suicide rates on reservations today are extremely high, as are poverty and lack of opportunity. There is a strong movement on reservations to restore the ancient spiritual traditions.

With polarization morphing into alienation in today's culture, the United States as a whole is experiencing similar feelings of anomie. What I have described in this chapter is traditional Native spirituality from my view, as a person not raised in the culture.

The Great Spiritual Culture Gap: Face Masks

When looking at Indigenous spiritual masks, do not accept your first impression if it is driven by a western perspective. Look again and seek to develop a partnership.

The way to approach a different culture's spirituality, such as their ceremonial masks, is to look for the humanity in them—and to remember that they are metaphorical. Try to feel the human emotion expressed in each mask. Remember we are discussing relationships, not objects.

There is more than what you see. For example, Seneca Face Society healing masks are carved out of the east side of a living tree, taking care not to harm the tree. If the carving started in the morning, the mask is painted red to reflect the sun's rays. If started in the afternoon, it is painted black to reflect the shadowed side of the tree. Some masks are only partially painted because they have a very specific function. The entire process demonstrates a complete unification of all that exists. Ego is not part of the cultural consciousness. Instead, the masks reflect the relationship of the carver to the tree, to the sun's rays, to a sense of being a part of the whole, and to the oneness of the universe.

Most non-Native people initially react to the masks negatively because they do not fit into Euro-American understanding in any way. Iroquois ceremonial masks reflect a wide range of human emotions, various Native stories, and the unique vision of each carver. Many masks also transition between ceremonial contexts, so there is an inherent fluidity in these masks that make them difficult to categorize. This aligns with the Native belief that spiritual powers move from one domain to another, placing them beyond human categorization. That is why, in Native spirituality, there is a creator, but no attempt is made to humanize, categorize, or explain that creator or those spiritual forces.

The keeper of Iroquois healing masks is always a woman, while those who use the mask are always men. The unification of the feminine and masculine flows through ceremony.

To perceive the reality the masks portray, one must draw upon an understanding that goes beyond everything written in this chapter—indeed, beyond everything written in this book.

Despite my years of passionate reading about Native America and forty years of personal involvement in Indigenous spirituality, explaining the meaning of the masks in English remains difficult. Spirituality is about experience that transcends explanation. I have read scholarly works, but it was not until I experienced Native spirituality that I found a pathway to the "knowing" understood in the ancient tradition and learned why only metaphor can come close to expressing those experiences. At the same time, I have learned to respect that path. I am still on the path and have not discovered the destination, nor do I wish to overanalyze or explain it.

The masks represent healing, but the Indigenous view of healing is holistic. Ceremony and the masks remind us that healing is physical, emotional, psychological, and spiritual. The masks reflect a holistic approach to community and transcend the need to define, categorize, and understand. They embody growth.

And as one matures, the masks will be seen differently even though they haven't changed. You have changed.

Bill Holm, in discussing Northwest Coast masks, pointed out:

> It is precisely because each piece was the creation of the mind of a man that it can be analyzed only superficially in terms of elements and principles, while that quality which raises the best of Northwest Coast design to the status of art remains unmeasured.
>
> Some of the most skillful artists of the southern Kwakiutl are also among the best dancers and song composers, a situation that probably was also true of the northern tribes during their heyday. (Holm, 2015, 93)

Mortuary Poles

Although you cannot tell from my painting on the next page, mortuary poles were wide enough in diameter to support a body. The deceased was placed at the top of a pole into which the family lineage had been carved. The inner part of the pole decayed first. Then the body, which had also decayed, collapsed into the

Haida mortuary poles in Haida Gwaii, Canada (Queen Charlotte Islands)

pole's interior. Eventually the pole fell, reuniting it with the earth as a natural process. New trees will sprout out of the "nurse logs" (fallen dead logs and human remains). The cycle of life continues into the eternal.

Walking in the Spirit

The Native holistic perspective envisions a deeper understanding of the unseen world—the world beyond the five senses. Indigenous ceremony without hierarchy, without an intermediary, focuses on the individual's personal experience as a part of a process. Metaphor in art, dance, and story embodies the flow of spirit. From the beauty of Momaday's words mentioned previously to the Iroquois masks, we witness a transcendence that surpasses human categorical definition.

Linear-binary Western thinking finds discomfort in that place where the holistic Indigenous thought resides. The natural world and its spiritual forces do not exist in categorized boxes. They reside in a natural flow. The contrast between Western and Indigenous thought is dramatically illustrated in two phrases, one Indigenous, "I am because we are," and one from the West, "I am the Resurrection." The distance the Western mind must travel to truly understand what it means to be Indigenous is vast—to see the Indigenous flow in masking, the Indigenous dance, the Indigenous heartbeat, and the Indigenous world of spirit.

CHAPTER 9

NATIVE AMERICAN CONTRIBUTIONS

Professor Jack Weatherford, DeWitt Wallace Professor of Anthropology at Macalester College, stated that Indigenous innovations "transformed the world." There are three reasons why:

1. An exchange of ideas throughout the hemisphere over thousands of years resulted in ongoing cultural diffusion.
2. Unlike other continents, the American hemisphere spans most of the earth's latitudes, creating multiple environmental conditions that affected agricultural development and hybridization.
3. As discussed in Chapter 3, Indigenous linguistics were foundational in a thought process that enabled new ideas and outcomes.

Few people realize the extent of Native American contributions in their lives. It is time to acknowledge them.

Agricultural Innovation

In 1492, the Indigenous cultures of this hemisphere were highly developed, while Europe was plagued with war, epidemics, starvation, and dictatorial governance—none of which existed in this hemisphere, with the exception of the expanding Inca Empire.

At that time, Native Americans cultivated over three hundred food crops, and many of these had dozens of variations that survived in a wide range of environmental conditions.

Today, as documented by Jack Weatherford in his book *Indian Givers*, three-fifths of the fruits and vegetables in cultivation were hybridized by Native America. The following foods were developed in Mexico and South, Central, and North America. All were unique to the American hemisphere. A partial list is shown on the next page.

Crop Adaptation

Native peoples also developed plants that thrived in different climates, with differing moisture levels, soil nutrients, and sun intensity. For example, in North America, corn varieties differed depending on whether they were grown in the drier climate of the Southwest or the moister climate of the Cahokia region, located in what is now western Illinois and eastern Missouri near modern day St. Louis. This reflected a deep understanding of their environment and its relationship to food production.

Native technology adjusted species to different environmental conditions. I remember, during a visit to the Peruvian Andes, walking through Quechuan (Inca) mountain village markets and seeing an incredible number of potato varieties. According to Weatherford (*Indian Givers*, 63), Native peoples of the Andes

Acorn	Cherimoya	Pine Nut
Agave	Chocolate	Potato (all kinds)
Allspice	Chokeberry	Prickly Pear
Amaranth	Concord (or Fox) Grapes	Pumpkin
American Blackberry	Corn (Maize)	Quinoa
American Ginseng	Cranberry	Sassafras
American Gooseberry	Elderberry	Squash (all kinds)
American Persimmon	Gooseberry	Sunflower Seeds
American Strawberry	Hazelnut	Sweet Potato
Arrowroot	Hickory nut	Sugar Apple (Sweetsop)
Avocado	Jerusalem Artichoke	Tamarillo (Tree tomato)
Beans (all kinds)	Jicama	Tapioca (Casava root)
Beechnut	Maple Syrup	Tomatillo (Musk Tomato)
Black Raspberry	Papaya	Tomato
Black Walnut	Passion Fruit	Vanilla
Blueberry	Pawpaw	White Sage
Brazil Nut	Peanut	Wild Ginger
Butternut	Pecan	Wild Rice (Manoomin)
Cashew	Peppers (all kinds except Black)	Wintergreen Mint
Chayote Squash	Pineapple	Yucca

produced 3,000 varieties of potatoes, in contrast to the 120 varieties grown today in North America, with only about twenty making up the majority of production.

Impact on European Health and Expansion

Euro-Americans tend to manipulate plant genetics and the environment to enhance crop production for the market. In contrast,

Native peoples hybridized the plants to fit the environment, making the foods they developed suitable for all European environments. This reduced famine in northern Europe and equalized the power between northern and southern European countries, such as England and Spain, relative to the economic theory of mercantilism. Eventually, Native American plants spread beyond Europe, improving the world's diet in both quantity and quality of foods.

Agricultural Relationships That Boosted Output

Native America did make some environmental changes, but they were guided by the rule of sustainability, never disrupting the natural processes of nature. In Central America and eastern and midwestern North America, a form of agricultural technology was developed that reflects Indigenous holistic thought, merging with the environment to produce sustainability while increasing productivity.

The Mayans in Central America called it the milpa, and it was a technique mainly used in forested areas in soils where high levels of vegetation competed for nutrients. It consisted of a field of small mounds about five to six inches high and one to two feet in diameter. Corn, beans, and squash were planted in each mound. Corn kernels were planted first in the center and squash seeds were planted on the edge. The squash leaves provided ground cover to prevent weeds. Once corn had grown three to five inches above the mound, beans were planted. The beans added nitrogen to the soil and their vines were supported by the corn stalks. The mounds were scattered around other natural vegetation along with large burned-off areas. Sunflowers were often planted along the edges of the garden area to provide both protection from insects and also seeds for consumption. This form of plant interrelationship greatly increased the productivity of each plant. Its importance was reflected in the Chapter 6 (Metaphor: The Mind That Sees in Relationship) stories of the three sisters.

In the 1930s, Euro-Americans replaced Native agricultural technology, which they called "hilling," with mono-crop planting, chemicals, and pesticides. This reduced the diversity of foods of Native origin and their nutritional value. That, in turn, led to depletion of the land's nutrients, its ability to support crop growth, and eventually led to the Dust Bowl in the plains, which was further intensified by changing weather conditions and the replacement of buffalo with cattle. This environmental destruction contrasts with the Native tendency to create variants that adjust to differing environments.

I participated in the maintenance of a Native garden in the Northland of the Kansas City Metropolitan area for more than 20 years. Thidaware Garden, a name from the Native peoples who once lived in the area, is located on an ancient Hopewell site in cooperation with the Kansas City Parks and Recreation Department. The garden includes Three Sisters crops (corn, beans, and squash) plus southwest Pueblo technology and seeds. I was amazed at the huge size of the squash leaves. I've often read how they protected the Three Sisters from weeds, but I had no idea how large and effective those leaves were until I was personally involved in that garden. Interestingly, the Pueblo corn has been hybridized to require less water than similar midwestern varieties. In the dryer climate of the Southwest, the Three Sisters technology is not used. The sources of water are nearby rivers such as the Rio Grande (which is now polluted with radiation from Los Alamos) or, in the case of the Arizona Hopis, rain.

Across the country, the different tribes adjusted their agriculture to their local environments. If this is of interest, I recommend reading the books on Indigenous agriculture found in the Bibliography.

American Democracy

Historians continue to attribute American Democracy to Athens, Rome, and the Magna Carta despite evidence to the contrary, and that bias is continuing into the 21st century, couched in racism and denial.

In fact, Native American governance heavily influenced our democracy. Thomas Paine, Ben Franklin, Roger Williams, along with European philosophers studied and worked to adopt many Native democratic values. See Chapter 4 for more on Native democracy.

Medicinal Plants and Medical Contributions

Native pharmacology was well developed in this hemisphere when Europeans arrived in the Americas. "From the very first contacts between the old world and the new world, European doctors recognized that the Indians held the key to the world's most sophisticated pharmacy. This cornucopia of new pharmaceutical agents became the basis for modern medicine and pharmacology" (Weatherford, 1998, 183–184).

Indigenous medicine reflected their relationship-oriented mentality, viewing nature as a close relative that provides the benefit of her medicinal properties.

As explained by Santee Dakota John Trudell, the true Native view is as follows: "All human beings are descendants of tribal people who were spiritually alive, intimately in love with the natural world, children of Mother Earth. When we were tribal people, we knew who we were, we knew where we were, and we knew our purpose. This sacred perception of reality remains alive and well in our genetic memory. We carry it inside of us, usually in a dusty box in the mind's attic, but it is accessible."

In other words, ancient Native American pharmacological knowledge was the birthplace of the present-day art of medicine and science of pharmacology.

Holistic Healing

In the Great Lakes regions, Native women had knowledge of approximately 300 herbal treatments for health problems. If the issue was beyond her knowledge, the family consulted a medicine person.

In the dry Southwest, Diné (Navajo) medicine people had about 3,000 herbal applications used for healing practices. The Diné had two categories of health practitioners: a diagnostician determined which specialty was needed for cure, and then sent the patient to a medical practitioner who specialized in that specific ailment. Sound familiar?

Native healing is holistic. It combines environmental pharmacological knowledge with mental, emotional, and spiritual healing. In the Indigenous view, causes of any given illness are also holistic and need a broad-based treatment.

When I visited Window Rock, Arizona, I was part of a tour group that visited a Diné woman healer. Without touching me or asking me any health questions, she diagnosed my asthma. She moved her hands above my body as I lay on the floor. That was all she did. The people I was with later told me my face turned bright red. Following this "simple" treatment, I had no asthma symptoms for the next six months. I did not have to use any of my prescribed asthma meds during that time.

Another experience occurred on the Pine Ridge Reservation, where I attended healing ceremonies and witnessed unexplainable healing. I saw a psychotic man from Vermont healed. The healer told him he could stop taking all medicines for his disorder. He returned about a year later and gave the medicine person a car to express his gratitude, explaining he no longer experienced psychotic delusions.

Other Major Contributions

Native contributions included the fields of architecture, art, astronomy, carpentry, ceramics, civil engineering, dentistry, environmental science, fiber/dyes/weaving, fishing, mathematics, medical knowledge and techniques, personal hygiene, and science.

See *American Indians Contributions to the World* in the Bibliography for the broader and more detailed list and for more specificity relative to tribal, linguistic, and geographic groups.

CHAPTER 10

FINDING NEW SOLUTIONS

... I also want to be remembered for emphasizing the fact that we have Indigenous solutions to our problems.

—Wilma Mankiller, Principal Chief,
Cherokee Nation of Oklahoma 1987–1995

Dangerous challenges threaten our country and our humanity. In looking for solutions, this book has examined two very different paradigms: Axial Effect nation-state patterns and tribalism.

We have a blind spot in our view of the past, anchored in the nation-state bias of defining progress in terms of technological and material development, and "power" as wealth, leverage, and control. We are raised to believe this without question.

But there is growing dissention and alienation in this country. The attack on the U.S. Capitol was part of a larger pattern that is eroding confidence in our systems. And people who do not feel safe are easier to manipulate.

"For now, one thing is clear: America's extremists are becoming more organized, more dangerous, and more determined, and they are not going away" (Walter, 160).

How We Got Here

The world of today inherited patterns that started with the formation of nation-states in ancient times. Those Axial patterns have rippled into the present, from ancient Greece and China to the Roman Empire, the Mongol Empire, European expansion and colonialism, World Wars I and II, and now Ukraine and Israel. Jamestown's theft of Native lands grew into seizing the entire hemisphere from Native peoples with the abstract ideological justification of "Manifest Destiny" (God's Will). And when colonists deboarded the first slaves from Africa in 1619, they planted the seed of slavery and expanded racism. Today, we see that egoic mentality of justification turning in on itself, a pattern repeated since ancient times, culminating in attempts to undermine our democracy.

We have two million people in U.S. prisons. The combination of law enforcement and imprisonment in 2019 cost U.S. taxpayers approximately $277 billion. That represents twenty-five percent of the world's incarcerated people with only 4.23% of the world's population.

Think of all the talent sitting in stagnation. This reminds me of Robert Franklin Stroud, known as the "Birdman of Alcatraz," who served a life sentence from 1909 until his death in 1963 for the murder of three people, one a prison guard. He was incarcerated at the Federal Penitentiary at Leavenworth, where he became a respected ornithologist, hence his nickname. While at Leavenworth, he made important contributions to the field of ornithology publishing two books, *Diseases of Canaries*, on the cure for hemorrhagic septicemia, and *Stroud's Digest on the Diseases of Birds*. When the U.S. Bureau of Prisons was created, Stroud was transferred to Alcatraz, ending his studies of ornithology. His work had already been acknowledged by professionals in the field as significant contributions to ornithology. While in Alcatraz, he expanded his knowledge into other fields, reading profusely.

So, why the violent behavior? A look at his childhood is informative. He grew up in Seattle with an alcoholic, abusive father, and a loving but self-absorbed mother. He left home at age 13 and lived on his own, supporting himself through various illegal activities before his incarceration. What if he had grown up in a nurturing environment? How would his story be different? And what more might he have contributed?

Today, there is a high rate of binge drinking and other drug use among high school students. Many suffer in attempts to cope with depression and loneliness despite being surrounded with fellow students and adults. So, what is missing? Is it just human nature to be depressed? Or is it a symptom that something in the social construct needs examination and correction? What is missing in a society so focused on objectification?

> *The most important thing each of us can know is our unique gift and how to use it in the world. Individuality is cherished and nurtured, because, in order for the whole to flourish, each of us has to be strong in who we are and carry our gifts with conviction, so they can be shared with others.*
> Robin Wall Kimmerer, *Braiding Sweetgrass*

From Hollywood movies to statements like "they were violent too," to "tomahawk chops" at the Kansas City Chiefs games, to virtually ignoring the original peoples of this land in our history classes, we have blocked their wisdom. Just as eighteenth-century Romanticist Samuel Taylor Coleridge wrote about casting the "light only on the bow of the ship," ignoring past wisdom, America has blocked the ability of Indigenous traditions to provide answers to today's problems.

Let's look deeper. Approximately twenty-three hundred years ago, Plato wrote:

> *Those who are able to see beyond*
> *the shadows and lies of their culture*
> *will never be understood, let alone*
> *believed, by the masses.*

What Is the Alternative?

Now consider the deceptively simple and more inclusive Native concept, "I am because we are." Its all-encompassing view challenges Plato's historic exclusivity common in nation-state observation and provides possible solutions for problems ranging from the environment to individual and international relationships.

Relationships were foundational to the Indigenous process of sustainability. Nurturing children into adulthood fostered that understanding. It was a state of being, not just an idea. It shifted the human mind to both emotional and intellectual knowing. In nurturing children, proper boundaries of behavior become self-internalized with a sense of personal responsibility. The individual saw the world as one inclusive entity in which we are all related to and responsible for its well-being.

Euro-Americans have never understood Indigenous cultures. At the root of their sense of superiority was a narrow definition of what qualifies as "civilized," which they defined materialistically, seeing the natural world in terms of its usefulness. They believed technological advances are the ultimate measure of human progress, and humans were above the rest of the natural world. Nature was non-living, something to be feared and used.

The following guideposts will not be easy, and they will take time. But as Abraham Lincoln said, "I'm a slow walker, but I never walk back."

It is time to walk forward.

Finding the Guideposts

Can we find a balance between the nation-state and tribal forms of human organization, sharing the benefits of each, with guardrails on human consumption, racism, and temptation toward corruption? It has never been done before. Is it possible now?

The world today tends to be reactive, addressing problems only after they have appeared. A shift from reactivity to an anticipatory, proactive approach is necessary for positive changes to occur. Achieving this will require tremendous effort. But the health of humanity and the planet are at stake. Daniel R. Wildcat echoed this sentiment when he said: "Historical and Ideological prejudices have continued to preclude serious examination of Indigenous knowledge that might help humankind address the current global environmental crisis" (2009, 37).

The primary Native values we must pay attention to are:

- Balance and harmony lead to sustainability.
- Humans are one part of a universal community. Respect for all others was fundamental.
- Egalitarian balance must occur between the feminine and masculine.
- The reconciliation of duality within life and nature is foundational.
- Nurturing children into adulthood, as opposed to controlling them is perhaps the most critical.
- Wealth of the soul is prioritized over material acquisition and leverage.

Of course, Native Americans were human—they were not free from violence. But discord was minimized because they:

- Viewed other tribes as part of the world community (in Lakota: Tun kan).
- Were socio-politically lineage-based—not border-based.
- Did not commoditize property.
- Were relationship orientated.
- Had a nurturing sense of community that made tribes less aggressive.

Now, let's consider how these values can strengthen our culture and ensure a better future.

The following list encapsulates ways to modify and improve today's accepted norms.

1. Raise Children to Self-Actualize

There can be no keener revelation of a society's soul than the way in which it treats its children.
—Nelson Mandela

It cannot be stressed enough: raising children in a nurturing environment is the foundation of a stable future. The authoritative methods of parental domination common in today's world invite disaster. That domination is at the root of the ego-driven mind, from the extreme self-centeredness of many politicians to our prisons full of inmates. As Frederick Douglass, American abolitionist, social reformer, writer, and statesman said, "It is easier to build strong children than to repair broken men."

Not everyone who grows up in a parent-dominated atmosphere ends up with an ego-driven personality—there are numerous experiential factors that mitigate those extremes. As Mahatma Gandhi said, "If we are to reach real peace in the world, we shall have to begin with the children."

A keen sense of personal identity is critical in healthy relationships and foundational both to communities and democracy. Nurturance is key to developing this identity, which strengthens relationships and open-minded communication. Traditional Native America believed that self-knowledge was the key to taking responsibility for oneself, community, balance, mature decision-making, a long-term perspective, and wisdom.

That level of interpersonal relationship is not found in the thousands of years of nation-state pyramidal development and societal class systems. This is why the concepts reflected in examples like the story of *Washaka* (Chapter 4), are critical in establishing societal sustainability.

Native cultures measured growth internally, within each person's maturation into adulthood and Elder. Raising children with a strong self-sense supported environmental sustainability. Children who are nurtured from the inside-out (being allowed to become who they are rather than being told who to be) do not have a hollow place inside that needs to be filled with materialism or addictions.

> *Many persons have a wrong idea of what constitutes true happiness. It is not attained through self-gratification but through fidelity to a worthy purpose.*
> —Helen Keller

The story of *Washaka* showed the process that allowed children to find and test their boundaries while protecting them from danger. Rose Fitzgerald Kennedy, mother of President John F. Kennedy, Senator and Attorney General Robert Kennedy, and Senator Ted Kennedy, understood that when she said, "I tried to allow my children to take risks, to test themselves."

2. Restructure American Education

One large-scale solution to counter the emergence of dysfunctional and dangerous human behavior can be accomplished in the education system. Schools need to revamp the entire curriculum from rote memory to critical thinking processes, and increase emphasis on the humanities, relationship-building, the arts, and how to differentiate between impartiality and bias in media—including social media. Additional suggestions include:

- Put aside the clock and calendar when making fundamental changes in education, child-rearing or democratizing government. This is a process in which progress dictates timing.
- Integrate K through 12 classes that are now taught separately (math, language arts, history, etc.), through team teaching. Life is not fragmentized. It flows like a river and so should these classes, to foster whole brain development and prevent linear-binary thinking. This will require training in collaboration because educators are accustomed to teaching in isolated classrooms and many have tried and given up on team teaching. That is why emphasis on process, not time, is important. When President Lincoln said, "I walk slowly, but I never walk back," he expressed an unwavering determination that is required for the challenges ahead.
- Introduce content that develops greater intercultural sensitivity in human relationships. For example, art appreciation would include art from diverse cultures, not just Western art. It could be introduced early in the educational system. To appreciate on some level is to connect.
- Shift from teacher-centered focus to student involvement in the process of learning. In my experience as an educator, schools focused first on what worked for teachers. I have seen schools give up too early on innovative ideas and fall back on what is familiar but less successful. Different processes take time, and modifications and refinement are always needed.
- Teach metaphor to develop whole brain intellect. Metaphor is

multi-layered. Metaphoric stories help individuals find different truths at different stages of their development. That is why metaphor was a key teaching component in Native America: it helped the individual self-actualize by finding their own understanding and path grounded in truth. It was a key part of nurturance that strengthened and unified the tribe.

- Structure classes to emphasize and strengthen our humanity. As a high school educator for thirty years, and an adjunct professor for another fourteen, I understand that this is not easy. But it can be accomplished with time and patience, including patience for oneself and respect for our personal humanity. For example, history should include the humanities instead of just a factual narrative of socio-political events enacted by the few. As Howard Zinn exemplified in his book, *The People's History of the United States,* manipulation by the "powerful" over the majority must change to a greater focus on our humanity.
- Provide parenting classes in schools and PTAs to educate and build nurturing parenting skills as opposed to the nation-state pattern of an outside-in approach. Nurturing children with an Indigenous inside-out process would reduce rebellious behavior.
- It's also time to integrate parents more effectively into the educational process. They should be an integral part of their child's education. Today's world of police-guarded schools with locked entry doors is a sign of serious societal decay, which is why it is more important than ever that the society becomes proactive in finding cures.
- Recognize multiple intelligences. Howard Gardner,

developmental psychologist and Harvard University Graduate School Professor of Cognition and Education, has identified nine types of human intelligence to reach a wider range of student intellect. They include visual-spatial, linguistic-verbal, logical-mathematical, bodily-kinesthetic, musical, interpersonal, intra-personal, naturalistic, and existential intelligences. To better serve students' multi-intelligences, schools need to recognize and address the above in their curriculum developments.

- Teach critical thinking, both inductive and deductive reasoning. Educational systems need to unify mind and action. There is an over-emphasis on goals, which only give direction. More emphasis should be placed on processes that incorporate the skills required to achieve the goals with critical thinking, fortitude, contextual knowledge, effort, and a sense of direction and focus. This process should begin as activities geared to age level in early elementary school and grow in sophistication throughout the educational process. Elementary students can learn how to see variables, options, and contradictions. As they grow toward high school, they can begin to formulate those options and variables into hypotheses and theories in problem solving.

Students should be taught to see failure as a guidepost that helps course-correct along the way.

By high school, they should be developing and testing hypotheses. For example, in a project to identify nation-state tendencies, once the research is completed, students should look at the process to identify the lessons it holds. Those findings should be single sentence generalized statements, in this case, naming nation-state tendencies. Educational processes should be geared to each student's individual maturation rate. See appendix for more detail.

All subjects, including critical thinking, the arts, and humanities, should hold equal position in curriculum decisions to develop whole brain thinking. This is more important than ever with the internet and social media introduction of AI and algorithms that often distort the truth and narrow the offered options, limiting the perspective.

- Educate our children to understand, value, and prioritize consensus building.
- Rewrite textbooks to tell the truth about history. Indigenous peoples and America as a whole deserve the truth.

3. Incorporate the Feminine View into Our Governmental System

This is imperative to the survival not only of our humanity but also our planet.

Native America understood that balancing the feminine and masculine qualities was a critical component in the decision-making process.

This is not just about gender, though women are desperately needed in governance. It is about a critical balance of sensitivity and practicality; foresight with immediacy; empathy and compassion with direct action. It is that which works toward unification, not from the top down, but from the bottom up, starting with the individual and extending to the whole. It all must come from what works naturally, not what is enforced, because it is all grounded in that strong sense of self-identity which is, by definition, tribalism.

Create Appropriate Support Structures

- Change our lifestyle to support the earth's ability to foster life. As Emma Marris pointed out in *Wild Souls*, "... humanity cannot simply shift agriculture and infrastructure around; we must learn to shrink it. We simply need to take up less space" (249–250).
- Accept and recognize that humans are part of nature. As part of the global community, we have an obligation to maintain the earth's sustainability.
- Redefine wealth and power to mean moral, ethical, and spiritual values and behavior. That begins in the schools and the parenting.
- Demand integrity and honesty in our leaders.
- Trace problems to their root causes. Do not accept superficial answers or define symptoms as the problems.
- Recognize and accept that America is changing, as it always has, due to immigration from other countries.
- Acknowledge the rights of the original peoples of this land and learn from them. This is a moral imperative. Ancient traditions must be taught and restored beginning in the parenting and education system on all reservations. There are already reservations where this is occurring such as the Akwesasne Kanien'kehaka (Mohawk) Freedom School in upstate New York.
- Use collaboration to identify and understand human differences. For example, Michigan Chief Tribal Court Judge Michael Petoskey (Grand Traverse Band of Ottawa and Chippewa) has restructured his courtroom using the ancient Indigenous process to focus on the community values of

"responsibility, relationship, reciprocity and respect." He did this by bringing together the families of aggrieved parties to create joint solutions in place of typical adversarial positioning centered on the individual.

- Where possible, apply W. Edwards Deming's model of bottom-up empowerment to governance and corporate structures in place of top-down pyramidal leadership design.

4. Restructure Socio-Political Organizations

Egotistical nation-state behavior wants to categorize everything. That is why the quote by Lord Acton (1834–1902), "Power tends to corrupt and absolute power corrupts absolutely," is such a relevant message for the 21st century.

There is an addictive quality to "power" as defined in materialistic, dominant terms. Additionally, the addiction and its negative consequences inevitably escalate. Nation-states are burdened with corruption and the issue of "too much and never enough," with little or no awareness of sustainability. Modern examples of this include:

- Territorial growth: Putin's attack on Ukraine.
- Governmental autocracy: Kim Jong Un's rule of North Korea.
- Economic expansion: U.S. strategic economic control and manipulation has replaced its historic territorial expansion, often at the expense of the environment.

After 5,000 years of nation-state socio-political constructs rising and falling, the world has reached an inflection point both in terms of catastrophic environmental disruption and potential power struggles. The patterns show that no top-down nation-state governmental structure is sustainable over time.

Reality is fluid and therefore relative. For example, some forms of conduct produce unity, while others create polarization. Feminine-masculine unification of mind is a key component in sustaining a socio-political organization through effective decision-making.

Given the tendency for pyramidal organizational structures to become corrupt, power must be redistributed. As difficult as this reorganization will be, survival of life on the planet is at stake. There is no longer room for argument and delay. Those addicted to power must yield to the well-being of all life on earth.

A synthesis of nation-state and tribal constructs may provide the pathway to global stability.

How do we begin to change that top-down pyramidal structure?

5. Embrace Consensus Building

The founding fathers did not propose a two-party system that would create divisiveness, although the seeds for that division already existed.

One flaw in our two-party system is the legislative process of voting "yea or nay," along with an internal power structure. That needs to stop. In its place, decision-making, whether in committee or in a legislature, should rely on a process of consensus building. Some have argued that it would be too slow. Would it be slower than what is happening in Congress now?

Before consensus building can begin, personal agendas driven by egotistical mentalities must be set aside; otherwise, consensus building will not work. Everyone in a governing body must prioritize community over their own political careers. Sometimes self-sacrifice is critical to the well-being of the whole. Consider the sacrifices Ukraine is making in order to survive. John F. Kennedy's book *Profiles in Courage* offers another inspiring example of people prioritizing community over self.

True democracies do not operate on "yea or nay" votes. They require that we see the humanity in others and genuinely care for the community. That is democracy "of the people." Not an electoral college. Not 51% of the people. All the people.

Before you write that off as impossible, remember that Native America did just that for twenty to thirty thousand years or more. And the population north of the Rio Grande before colonization is estimated to have been twenty million.

Three factors are critical in consensus-building democracies.

1. The population, as children, must grow through a nurturing process as discussed earlier. Nurturing develops individuals with a strong self-identity who do not need an egoic mentality to bolster their self-confidence. People who are nurtured automatically connect to that sense of oneness. It does not have to be taught or imagined. It is just a part of reality.
2. As previously mentioned, the educational process must engage the whole brain, including critical thinking, problem-solving, and the arts.
3. Our government must be balanced with egalitarian feminine/masculine representation following the Indigenous model. Native America understood that a feminine-masculine balance was a critical part in the decision-making process.

This trifecta of characteristics developed individuals who made decisions based on a strong sense of self in relationship to community and a broad base of criteria for consideration. Today, community well-being is often subjugated to decisions based on "power" and materialistic economic health and wealth.

We are at an inflection point. Nixon shifted us in that direction, and we have since moved to the brink. If we do not end the addiction to materialistic power, we will become an autocracy. The seeds were planted in the colonial period. Though that may seem like a long time ago, it is brief compared to the 5,000-year history of nation-states. That is 5,000 years of repeated, failed historic patterns. It is time for our history classes to explore pre-nation-state development more deeply, as that is where our humanity resides.

The reforms mentioned above represent conceptual starting points with the idea they will be adapted and refined contextually as development is underway. The opportunity on the local level for creative ideas is endless, and its potential is limited only by the human imagination, emerging out of balanced feminine and masculine perspectives that allow everyone to speak without time limits or interruption. The goal of these local committees is creativity not limited by interval time (the hands of the clock), giving us time to develop socio-political systems that work and guarantee each individual's development to fuller potential and passion.

6. Challenge Racism

Racism is a major obstacle to local control and individual destiny. It uses fear to maintain power in the pyramidal structure.

There is an absurdity to racial antagonism based on the amount of melanin in one's skin. Prehistorically, that was caused by exposure to the sun's rays. Racism is a holdover from this country's inhumane acts of slavery and of aggressively and violently stealing Indigenous land. Racism is a nail in the coffin of our humanity and future survival.

> *Where justice is denied, where poverty is enforced, where ignorance prevails, and where any one class is made to feel that society is in an organized conspiracy to oppress, rob, and degrade them, neither persons nor property will be safe.*
> —Frederick Douglass

Racial justice and equality must coexist for human decency. Sustainability is not possible without justice and equality for all people, including people of color. True democracy cannot exist without acknowledging and healing the wounds of the past.

In the late 1970s, I did post-graduate work at Stanford University. There was a Hispanic educator in my class from the Los Angeles area. She described that every year after harvest season, U.S. Immigration authorities showed up at her school checking Latina and Latino students for proof of citizenship. Children who could not present proof were taken from the classroom and loaded onto buses heading south of the border. Frantic parents would show up at school looking for their missing children.

It is obvious why these agents came just after wealthy landowners had paid emigrants atrociously low harvest-season wages. A society that engages in such ego-driven, self-interested, and discriminatory behavior is a self-destructive society.

The solutions for ending racism in America reside in two areas: parenting and the educational system.

Racial injustice will not end until we develop nurturing child-rearing practices and improve our educational system. It will also not end until we replace materialism with human decency and value relationships above profiteering.

A thorough examination of Indigenous socio-political organizations would assist in finding solutions to our current human-rights issues. The various confederated tribal structures provide guidance when legitimate scholars explain the internal operations of their democracies. Some are offered in the Bibliography of this book. Consult Iroquois and other Native scholars on their own history. Information and guidelines are available.

It is critical to take this information seriously and change our system to serve the people instead of a power structure.

7. Reverse the Citizens United v FEC Supreme Court Decision

Decision-making cannot simply focus on economics. Consider the Citizens United v FEC Supreme Court decision. It gave corporations the rights of citizens, ending campaign contribution limits by proclaiming them to be a violation of the first amendment right of free speech. Citizens United has enabled wealthy individuals and special interest groups to covertly influence elections with dark money. This infringement on our rights must end.

Corporations are not people. Their goal is profit, without the consideration of human rights. They do not have a conscience. They do not have families whose futures matter to them and influence their decisions. Employees are considered objects.

The reforms outlined above may appear impossible and idealistic. Perhaps they are. But 5,000 years should provide adequate evidence that we need to broaden our view going forward. Today, our tunnel vision is a source of human disaster.

8. Eliminate the Electoral College

Hillary Clinton won the popular vote in the 2016 presidential election by almost 2.9 million votes, which represented 48.2% of the voting public versus Trump's 46.1%. This reflected the will of the people of the United States. The results of the Electoral College were not aligned with the popular vote, resulting in Donald Trump being named president.

In all other U.S. elections, candidates are elected by popular vote of the citizens. The election of the president and vice president are the exceptions to this process. It is time for the Electoral College to be removed from the process and for the president and vice president of the United States to be elected by the voting public alone. This is critical to the fundamental meaning of the word "democracy."

Becoming the Best That We Can Be

What enables humanity to flourish? What brings out the worst in us?

It is time to take a serious look at these questions and realize that each person can make a difference. A look at Native American tribalism, with its egalitarian socio-political systems, nurturing of children, spirituality, and ethos, could lead not only to our survival but also to a much more fulfilling lifestyle.

There are four foundational areas that must be brought back into our societies, into our consciousness. We must:

1. Reconnect to the natural world to rediscover our humanity.
2. Re-establish egalitarianism between women and men, between feminine and masculine energy and the universe.
3. Learn how to parent our children through an inside-out process of nurturing.
4. Revamp our educational system toward whole brain thought and away from the emphasis on linear-binary thinking.

The re-establishment of our human dignity depends on achieving these four goals. In the process, our relationships must replace objectification, and we must reduce our dependence on product consumption. We must put "civil" back into "civilization."

If drastic and difficult measures are not taken, Albert Einstein's grim prediction may become reality: "I don't know with what weapons World War III will be fought, but World War IV will be fought with sticks and stones."

Focusing on human relationships may be much more fulfilling than property accumulation and job advancement.

At 86 years old, as I look back to growing up in that 10-story building listening to Charlie "Yardbird" Parker and Count Basie jazz and talking on that black "daffodil" phone technology, it appears to me our lives have not gotten easier, they have only become more complicated by technology.

The "progress" we've made is an illusion. When we ignore sustainability and prioritize external material development over internal personal growth, we do not truly progress. Only by improving upon our humanity can we move forward.

The Time to Act Is Now

These thoughts take me back to the popular protest music of the 1960s. Songwriter and singer Pete Seeger composed many songs, one of his most popular being "Where Have All the Flowers Gone?" In the lyrics, Seeger poses the question, "When will they ever learn?" Singer Joan Baez sang Seeger's song "We Shall Overcome," which became one of the most popular songs for minorities at the time.

As singers Peter, Paul, and Mary asked in the song "Blowin' in the Wind," composed by Bob Dylan, "How many times can a man turn his head and pretend he just doesn't see … How many ears must one man have before he can hear people cry."

The lyrics of songs from the 1960s emotionally captured the spirit of the times, reflecting the anti-war movements and the demand for racial equality and justice. Those songs are just as cogent today. The answers are there, "Blowin' in the Wind." We just have to make ourselves aware.

We must be patient as progress is slow, but we should never walk back as President Lincoln pointed out. It is okay to be a slow walker. We just need to take the next right step.

The time to explore possibilities and find real, long-term solutions is now. However, to achieve this, we must look deeper to identify the root causes of our problems.

Our children's future is at stake. As Lakota leader Sitting Bull (Tatanka Iyotake) so eloquently said in the 19th century: "Let us put our minds together and see what life we can make for our children."

APPENDIX

CRITICAL THINKING PARADIGM

Broadly speaking, learning is a lifelong process that does not end with formal education. Critical thinking employs both inductive and deductive processes to enhance clarity and accuracy. It is an important discipline that aids in growth and self-actualization.

The critical thinking process contains the following elements:

- Learn basic facts of the subject or events.
- Clarify the issues you are investigating.
- Develop possible hypotheses (a tentative inference generated for the purpose of testing) or explanations.
- Gather facts from dependable sources that help test the validity of those hypotheses.
- Differentiate between inconclusive (contextual) and conclusive (factual) evidence.
- Develop and evaluate conclusions.
- Continue to evaluate as new evidence is encountered.

Hypotheses must:

- Provide an obvious answer to the problem or issues you are analyzing.
- Hold up to the test of validity.
- Be stated as a single sentence containing one idea to provide clear direction in research.

In doing the research, you must:

- Understand the difference between inconclusive evidence (evidence that is valid but contextual—not factual) and conclusive evidence (facts).
- Examine cursory (surface) sources and definitive (deep, clearly defined) sources.
- Differentiate between primary and secondary sources of information.
- Keep the relevant information and discard the irrelevant information.
- Never rely on a single source of information. Always seek supporting information.
- Include different forms of observation: info from surveys, audio-visual materials, interviews, and all other forms of observation.

Conclusion is a simple summary of the research results.

Extrapolate principles that follow from the information. These principles should help proactively predict outcomes before an event materializes. The purpose of creating generalizations is to shift from a reactive to proactive thought process.

Social Science generalizations:

- Are stated in complete sentences.
- Eliminate time and space barriers (stated as rules of human behavior—not just a time-specific event or tendency).
- Are not 100% predictable but can have a high degree of probability when the process is done correctly. Think in terms of tendencies or proclivities.
- Should generate new meaning, understanding, and impact.

BIBLIOGRAPHY

Adair, Mary. *Prehistoric Agriculture in the Central Plains.* University of Kansas Publications in Anthropology, 1988.

Alexie, Sherman. *The Toughest Indian in the World.* Grove Press, 2000.

Angarova, Galina, Executive Director. "We Have Always Been Here: Decolonizing Gender." *Cultural Survival Quarterly* (December 2022).

Arden, Harvey, and Steve Wall. *Travels in a Stone Canoe: The Return to the Wisdom Keepers.* Simon and Schuster, 1998.

Axtell, James. *The European and the Indian: Essays in the Ethnohistory of Colonial North America.* Oxford University Press, 1981.

Bailey, Garrick, and Daniel C. Swan. *Art of the Osage.* St. Louis Art Museum in Association with the University of Washington Press, 2004.

Barreiro, Jose, ed. *Indian Roots of American Democracy.* Akwe:kon Press, Cornell University, 1992.

Bateson, Gregory. *Steps to an Ecology of Mind.* University of Chicago Press, 2000. First published by Ballantine Books in 1972.

Bell, Eve. *An Apache Odyssey: Indeh.* University of Oklahoma Press, 1980.

Ben-Ghiat, Ruth. *Strongmen: Mussolini to the Present.* W. W. Norton & Co., 2021.

Berkhofer, Jr., Robert F. *White Man's Indian, The: Images of the American Indian from Columbus to the Present*. Alfred A. Knopf, 1978.

Berlo and Phillips. *Native North American Art*. Oxford University Press, 1998.

Bigby, Bobbie Chaw. "Colonialism, Capitalism, and Climate Change." *Cultural Survival Quarterly*, June 2023.

Binford, Lewis R. *Constructing Frames of Reference: An Analytical Method for Archeological Theory Building Using Ethnographic and Environmental Data Sets*. University of California Press, 2019.

Bixcul, Bryan. "Indigenous Peoples are Again Sidelined in Major Decisions at COP 27." *Cultural Survival Quarterly* (March 2023).

Blackhawk, Ned. *The Rediscovery of America: Native Peoples and the Unmaking of U.S. History*. Yale University Press, 2023.

Blackhawk, Ned. *Violence Over the Land*. Harvard University Press, 2006.

Blattman, Christopher. *Why We Fight: The Roots of War and the Paths to Peace*. University of Chicago Press, 2023.

Bol, Marsha C. *North South East West: American Indians and the Natural World*. Carnegie Museum of Natural History and Roberts Rinehart Publishers, 1998.

Bolen, Anne. "The Bedrock of Pamunkey People." *American Indian Journal: National Museum of the American Indian* (Spring 2023).

Bray, Kingsley M. *Crazy Horse: A Lakota Life*. University of Oklahoma Press, 2006.

Brody, J. J., and Rina Swentzell. *To Touch The Past: The Painted Pottery of the Mimbres People*. Hudson Hills Press, 1996.

Brooks, Geraldine. *Caleb's Crossing*. Penguin Books, 2011.

Bruchac, Joseph. *Turtle Meat and Other Stories*. Holy Cow! Press, 1992.

Caduto, Michael J., and Joseph Bruchac. *Keepers of the Earth: Native American Stories and Environmental Activities for Children*. Fulcrum Publishing, 1997.

Caduto, Michael J. and Joseph Bruchac. *Native American Gardening: Stories, Projects and Recipes for Families*. Fulcrum Publishing, 1996.

Child, Brenda J. *Holding Our World Together: Ojibwe Women and the Survival of Community*. Penguin Books, 2013.

Colwell, Chip. *Plundered Skulls and Stolen Spirits: Inside the Fight to Reclaim Native America's Culture*. University of Chicago Press, 2017.

Commager, Henry Steele. *The Empire of Reason: How Europe Imagined and America Realized the Enlightenment*. Doubleday, 1978.

Cronon, William. *Changes in the Land: Indians, Colonists, and the Ecology of New England.* Hill and Wang, 1983.

Custalow, Dr. Linwood "Little Bear," and Angela L. Daniel "Silver Star." *Original Politics: Making America Sacred Again*. SelectBooks, Inc., 2020.

Custalow, Dr. Linwood "Little Bear," and Angela L. Daniel "Silver Star." *The True Story of Pocahontas: The Other Side of History*. Fulcrum Publishing, 2007.

Deloria, Jr., Vine. *God is Red: A Native View of Religion*. Fulcrum Publishing, 1992.

Deloria, Jr., Vine. *Red Earth, White Lies: Native Americans and the Myth of Scientific Fact*. Scribner, 1995.

Deloria, Jr., Vine, and Daniel R. Wildcat. *Power and Place: Indian Education in America*. Fulcrum Resources, 2001.

Divina, Fernando and Marlene Divina. *Foods of the Americas: Native Recipes and Traditions*. Ten Speed Press in Association with Smithsonian National Museum of the American Indian, 2004.

Dubin, Lois Sherr. *North American Indian Jewelry and Adornment: From Prehistory to the Present*. Harry N. Abrams, Inc., 1999.

Dunbar-Ortiz, Roxanne. *An Indigenous Peoples' History of the United States*. Beacon Press, 2014.

Erdrich, Louise. *The Antelope Wife*. HarperCollins Publishers, Inc., 1998.

Erdrich, Louise. *The Night Watchman*. Harper Perennial, 2020.

Evans, Tony Tekaroniake. "Native Negotiations are a Winning Alternative to Courts." *American Indian Journal: National Museum of the American Indian* (Fall 2023).

Faden, Ray (Tehanetorens). *Legends of the Iroquois*. Book Publishing Co., 1998.

Farella, John. *The Wind in a Jar*. University of New Mexico Press, 1993.

Fenton, William N. *The False Faces of the Iroquois.* University of Oklahoma Press, 1990.

Fritz, Gayle J. *Feeding Cahokia: Early Agriculture in the*

North American Heartland. The University of Alabama Press, 2019.

Grinde, Jr., Donald A. and Johansen, Bruce E. *Exemplar of Liberty: Native America and the Evolution of Democracy*. American Indian Studies Center, University of California, 2008.

Hari, Johann. *Stolen Focus: Why You Can't Pay Attention and How to Think Deeply Again*. Random House, 2022.

Harjo, Joy. *An American Sunrise: Poems*. W.W. Norton, Inc., 2019.

Holm, Bill. *Northwest Coast Indian Art: An Analysis of Form*. University of Washington Press, 2015.

Irwin, Louis Two Ravens and Robert Liebert. *Two Ravens: The Life and Teachings of a Spiritual Warrior*. Destiny Books, 1996.

Johnson, Broderick H., ed. *Navajo Stories of the Long Walk Period*. Diné Press, 1973.

Keoke, Emory Dean, and Kay Marie Porterfield. *American Indian Contributions to the World: 15,000 Years of Inventions and Innovations*. Checkmark Books, 2003.

Kimmerer, Robin Wall. *Braiding Sweetgrass: Indigenous Wisdom, Scientific Knowledge, and the Teachings of Plants*. Milkweed Editions, 2013.

Kovach, Margaret. *Indigenous Methodologies: Characteristics, Conversations, and Contexts*. University of Toronto Press, 2009.

Krenak, Edson. "Indigenous Peoples Are Essential to The Rights of Nature." *Cultural Survival Quarterly* (September 2022).

Lee, Jamie. *Washaka the Bear Dreamer: A Lakota Story Based on Leon Hale's Dream*. Many Kites Press, 2006.

Levin, Aaron. "In the Fading Tracks of Caribou." *American Indian Journal: National Museum of the American Indian* (Winter 2022).

Lyons, Oren et al., *Exiled in the Land of the Free: Democracy, Indian Nations and the U.S. Constitution*. Clear Light Publishers, 1992.

Mann, Charles C. *1491: New Revelations of the Americas Before Columbus*. Vintage Books Edition, a Division of Random House, 2011.

Mann, Charles C. *1493: Uncovering the New World Columbus Created*. First Vintage Books Edition, a Division of Random House, 2011.

Marris, Emma. *Wild Souls*. Bloomsbury Publishing, 2021.

Mathews, John Joseph. *The Osages: Children of the Middle Waters*. University of Oklahoma Press, 1982.

McDonnell, Michael A. *Masters of Empire: Great Lakes Indians and the Making of America*. Hill and Wang, A Division of Farrar, Straus and Giroux, 2015.

McMaster, Gerald, and Clifford E. Trafzer, eds. *Native Universe: Voices of Indian America*. National Museum of the American Indian, Smithsonian Institution, in Association with National Geographic, 2004.

Mehrabian, Dr. Albert. *Silent Messages: Implicit Communication of Emotions and Attitudes*. Wadsworth, 1981.

Mihesuah, Devon A. *Indigenous American Women:*

Decolonization, Empowerment, Activism. University of Nebraska Press, 2003.

Mihesuah, Devon A., and Elizabeth Hoover, eds. *Indigenous Food Sovereignty in the United States: Restoring Cultural Knowledge, Protecting Environment, and Regaining Health*. University of Oklahoma Press, 2019.

Momaday, N. Scott. *House Made of Dawn*. Harper and Row, 1968.

Momaday, N. Scott. *The Man Made of Words: Essays, Stories, Passages*. St. Martin's Press, 1997.

Moulard, Barbara L. *Within the Underworld Sky: Mimbres Ceramic Art in Context*. Twelvetrees Press Inc., 1981.

Namias, June. *White Captives: Gender and Ethnicity on the American Frontier*. University of North Carolina Press, 1995.

National Park Service. *Hopewell Culture*. National Historical Park, U.S. Department of Interior

Native American Expressive Culture, Akwe:kon Press, Fulcrum Publishing, 1995.

"Navajo Ceremonial Basket Interpretations," Natural History Museum of Utah, accessed September 30, 2024.

Nerburn, Kent. *The Girl Who Sang to the Buffalo: A Child, an Elder and the Light from an Ancient Sky*. New World Library, 2013.

Nerburn, Kent. *Neither Wolf Nor Dog: On Forgotten Roads with an Indian Elder*. New World Library, 2012.

Nerburn, Kent. *Wolf at Twilight: An Indian Elder's Journey Through a Land of Ghosts and Shadows*. New World Library, 2009.

Ortiz, Simon J., ed. *Beyond the Reach of Time and Change: Native American Reflections on the Frank A. Rinehart Photograph Collection*. University of Arizona Press, 2004.

Parry, Glen Aparicio. *Original Thinking: A Radical Revisioning of Time, Humanity, and Nature*. North Atlantic Books, 2015.

Peat, F. David. *Blackfoot Physics: A Journey into the Native American Universe*. Phanes Press, 2002.

Penney, David and George C. Longfish. *Native American Art*. Hugh Lauter Levin Assoc., Inc., 1994.

Perdue, Theda. *Cherokee Women: Gender and Culture Change, 1700–1835*. University of Nebraska Press, 1998.

Pritchard, Evan T. *No Word for Time: The Way of the Algonquin People*. Council Oak Books, LLC, 2001.

Rabb, J. Douglas, and Dennis H. McPherson. *Indian from the Inside: A Study in Ethno-metaphysics*. The Centre for Northern Studies, Lakehead University, 1993.

Radin, Paul. *Winnebago Hero Cycles*. Waverly Press, 1948.

Radin, Paul. *The Winnebago Tribe*. University of Nebraska Press, 1973.

Raff, Jennifer. *Origin: A Genetic History of the Americas*. Hachette Book Group, 2022.

Randall, Lisa. *Warped Passages: Unraveling the Mysteries of the Universe's Hidden Dimensions*. Ecco, An Imprint of HarperCollins Perennial, 2006.

Richardson, Heather Cox. *Wounded Knee: Party Politics and the Road to An American Massacre*. Basic Books, 2010.

Richter, Daniel K. *Before the Revolution: America's Ancient Past*. Belknap Press of Harvard University Press, 2011.

Richter, Daniel K. *Facing East From Indian Country: A Native History of Early America*. Harvard University Press, 2003.

Richter, Daniel K. *The Ordeal of the Longhouse: The Peoples of the Iroquois League in the Era of European Colonization.* University of North Carolina Press, 1992.

Richter, Daniel K., and James H. Merrell. *Beyond the Covenant Chain: The Iroquois and Their Neighbors in Indian North America, 1600–1800*. Pennsylvania State University Press, 2003.

Roberts, David. *Once They Moved Like the Wind: Cochise, Geronimo, and the Apache Wars*. Simon and Schuster, 1994.

Roosevelt III, Kermit. *The Nation That Never Was: Reconstructing America's Story*. University of Chicago Press, 2022.

Rowen, Andrew. *Encounters Unforeseen: 1492 Retold.* All Persons Press, 2017.

Schmookler, Andrew Bard. *The Parable of Tribes: The Problem of Power in Social Evolution.* State University of New York Press, 1995.

Schumacher, Ernst Friedrich. *Small is Beautiful*. Harper Collins, 2010.

Seaver, James E., and June A. Namias, eds. *A Narrative of the Life of Mrs. Mary Jemison.* University of Oklahoma Press, 1992.

Segal, Charles M., and David C. Stineback. *Puritans, Indians & Manifest Destiny*. G. P. Putnam's Sons, 1977.

Shannon, Timothy J. *Iroquois Diplomacy on the Early American Frontier*. Penguin Group, 2009.

Sharp, Jay W. "Cochise and the Bascom Affair." https://www.desertusa.com/ind1/Cochise.html

Silko, Leslie Marmon and Larry McMurtry. *Ceremony.* Penguin Books, 2006.

Smith, Erminnie A. *Myths of the Iroquois. Smithsonian Institute-Bureau of Ethnology*, 1983.

Snyder, Timothy D. *On Tyranny: Twenty Lessons from the Twentieth Century*. Penguin Random House, 2017.

Speck, Dara Culhane. *An Error in Judgement: The Politics of Medical Care in an Indian/White Community*. TalonBooks, 1987.

Stannard, David E. *American Holocaust: The Conquest of the New World.* Oxford University Press, 1992.

Steeves, Paulette F. C. The Indigenous Paleolithic of the Western Hemisphere. University of Nebraska Press, 2021.

Swentzell, Roxanne and Patricia M. Perea, eds. *Pueblo Food Experience Cookbook: Whole food of Our Ancestors*. Museum of New Mexico Press, 2016.

Tarnas, Richard. "A Brief History of Western Thought." Youtube, uploaded by ArchetypalView, 19/10/2012.

Tarnas, Richard. *The Passion of the Western Mind: Understanding the Ideas That Have Shaped Our World View*. Ballantine Books, 1993.

Tingle, Tim. *Walking the Choctaw Road*. Cinco Puntos Press, 2003.

Trautmann, Rebecca Head. "Women as Leaders and Nurturers." *American Indian Journal: National Museum of the American Indian* (Fall 2022).

von Petzinger, Genevieve. *The First Signs: Unlocking the Mysteries of the World's Oldest Symbols*. Atria Books, 2016.

Wade, Edwin L., ed. *The Arts of the North American Indian, Native Traditions in Evolution*. Hudson Hill Press, in association with Philbrook Art Center, Tulsa, 1986.

Walker, James R., Raymond J. DeMallie, ed., and Elaine A. Jahner, ed. *Lakota Belief and Ritual*. University of Nebraska Press, 1980.

Walker, James R., Raymond J. DeMallie, ed., and Elaine A. Jahner, ed. *Lakota Myth*. University of Nebraska Press, 1983.

Wallace, Paul A. W. *The White Roots of Peace*. The Chauncy Press, 1986.

Walter, Barbara F. *How Civil Wars Start and How to Stop Them*. Crown Publishing: Penguin Random House, 2022.

Ward, Jacob. *The Loop: How Technology is Creating a World without Choices and How to Fight Back*. Hachette Book Group, 2022.

Weatherford, Jack. *Indian Givers: How the Indians of North America Transformed the World*. Crown Publishers, Inc., 1998.

Weil, Zoe. *The World Becomes What We Teach: Educating a Generation of Solutionaries*. Lantern Publishing & Media, 2021.

Whiteford, Andrew Hunter. *North American Indian Arts*. Golden Press and Western Publishing Co., Inc., 1973.

Whitehat, Sr., Albert. *Life's Journey—Zuya: Oral Teachings from Rosebud*. University of Utah Press, 2012.

Wilbur, Matika. *Project 562: Changing the Way We See Native America*. Ten Speed Press, 2023.

Wildcat, Daniel. *Red Alert: Saving the Planet with Indigenous Knowledge*. Fulcrum Publishing, 2009.

Young Bear, Severt, and R. D. Theisz. *Standing in the Light: A Lakota Way of Seeing*. University of Nebraska Press, 1994.

Zinn, Howard. *A People's History of the United States: 1492–Present*. Harper Perennial Modern Classics, 1999.

ABOUT THE AUTHOR

Gil Nichols is a lifelong student of North American Indian cultures. He was adopted by an Ihanktonwan (Lake Andes) Dakota family and has participated in Lakota and Dakota tribal ceremonies for more than 40 years, including the Sundance, five *hamblecias* (vision quests), and numerous Inipi (purification ceremonies) and healing ceremonies.

Gil earned a BS in Education from University of Central Missouri and a Master of Education from the University of Missouri-Columbia. He did post-graduate work at Western Oregon University, Western Michigan University, Santa Clara University, Stanford University and the University of Missouri-Kansas City.

For 30 years, Gil taught high school social sciences where he developed a critical thinking curriculum model for his classes. After retiring, he taught American Indian Studies at William Jewell College and the University of Missouri-Kansas City for 14 years. He has also taught Osher classes (University of Kansas) and *SPARK classes*, a similar organization offered through University of Missouri-Kansas City, and served as a tour guide at the Nelson-Atkins Museum of Art.

He volunteered with Native American prison inmates at both Kansas State Penitentiary in Lansing, Kan. and Federal U.S. Penitentiary in Leavenworth, Kan. For seven years, he helped arrange native inmate programs in the prisons, including native guest speakers. He also conducted training for the Central States U.S. Parole Commissioner and Staff in Native American cultures.

Gil was active for many years in the leadership of the Thidaware Native American Association at Line Creek Community Center in Kansas City.

He has traveled extensively to reservations across the country and has a collection of historic and contemporary Native American art. He has also traveled internationally to India, Egypt, Peru, Europe, Turkey, and Morocco. He resides in Kansas City, Mo.

www.ingramcontent.com/pod-product-compliance
Lightning Source LLC
Chambersburg PA
CBHW070107030426
42335CB00016B/2052
9781965278321